Bonnie COOKS!

BITS & BOBS & ANTELOPE TOES

Bonnie Hyatt-Murphy

PHOTOGRAPHS BY TOM MURPHY

Crystal Creek Press

www.tmurphywild.com

DEDICATION

This cookbook is dedicated to Laurence and Lillian Griffith, my grandparents, who valued wonderful food and good conversation.

Tom Murphy, my husband and companion, who always asks, "Is it chocolate?"

Don and Clarice Walters, who have shared their most treasured recipes, with generosity and love.

Amber Twiford, my niece, for untold hours of typing.

Copyright © 2009 by Bonnie Hyatt-Murphy
Photographs © 2009 by Tom Murphy

Published by Crystal Creek Press
402 South 5th, Livingston, Montana 59047

ISBN 1-931832-03-X

Cataloging-in-Publication data is on file at the Library of Congress.

Content design by Tracey Jones, Bozeman, Montana

This cookbook would not have been possible without all the recipes submitted by our family, and friends. Third edition 2009. Thank you.

I love to cook, having grown up in a huge extended family in Iowa, where sweet corn was cooked in a blue open canner. I always think big when I think food. It was natural then, when I took up cooking for my husband's photographic workshops, that I would enjoy producing quantities of good food for groups from around the country. I rely a good deal on the common sense of my Grandmother Griffith's cooking methods. (If she ever had a cup measure, I never saw it.) This means cooking mainly by your nose, your eye for the quantities, the feel of the dough in your hands, and the freshness of the ingredients. In our business people always ask me how I learned to cook, and I must admit my only qualification is that I ate abundantly of excellent food my entire childhood. This cookbook represents the many recipes prepared for and eaten mainly on the snowbanks of Yellowstone Park. All have been enjoyed by people half freezing from the cold of a Yellowstone winter, outdoors along the Gardner River, or at the confluence of Soda Butte Creek and the Lamar River, magical places.

For the purposes of clarity, I have added cup measures and a real tablespoon and teaspoon. When I know the origin of the recipe, I have given credit to the person who gave it to me, accompanied by a description of that person.

I am proposing this cookbook for all those people out there who still understand the Montana madness to which people succumb when they visit us out here. We get a call nearly every day from somebody homesick for Montana. This includes the people who have never set foot in our beautiful valleys or hiked by our blue ribbon streams. It is my intention that by providing them with an anecdotal Montana cookbook, they can have fun visiting here through the foods, the people, and the gatherings of our region.

CONTENTS

Nibbles 2

Breads & Rolls 10

Breakfast Specialties 24

Cakes & Cookies 38

Pies & Desserts 75

Salads & Dressings 90

Vegetables 106

Entrees 111

Soups 129

Sauces 141

Bits & Bobs 145

NIBBLES

ARTICHOKE AND TARRAGON DIP

2 6 oz. jars marinated artichoke
   hearts (drained and chopped)
1/2 cup mayonnaise
1/2 cup sour cream
1/2 cup grated Romano cheese
1 tablespoon dried tarragon

Bake dip until heated at 350 in a 3 cup souffle dish - 30 minutes.

CRAB MEAT PARMESAN CANAPES

12 slices white bread, crusts
   discarded, and bread cut in 4
   triangles
1 cup fresh crab meat
2/3 cup mayonnaise
2/3 cup parmesan cheese
2 scallions, chopped fine
1 teaspoon fresh lemon juice

Toast bread on baking sheet in 400 degree oven until golden, about 5 min.

Bake assembled crab meat toasts in middle of oven until puffed, 350 degrees for 10 minutes.

APRICOT BRANDIED BRIE

1 round Brie
1 cup apricot preserves
3/4 cup Brandy (Mandarin Napoleon)

Cut a fresh loaf baguette into 1/2" slices.
Use red grapes to garnish.
Let Brie come to room temperature, prick with fork.
Mix preserves and brandy, heat but don't boil-pour hot mixture over brie, and serve with baguette slices.

BEEF BITES

1/3 cup soy sauce
2 tablespoons honey
1/2 teaspoon ground ginger
1 clove garlic, crushed
1 teaspoon grated onion
1/2 cup red wine
1 can water chestnuts

Mix all together.
Cut a sirloin steak in strips, marinate at least one hour in the mixture. Wrap marinated meat around a water chestnut.

Broil 3-4 minutes on oven rack about 5"- 8" from the heat.

BBQ DRUMETTES

2 cups water
1 cup soy sauce
1 cup sherry
1/2 cup brown sugar
1/3 cup chopped green onions

Simmer together for about 45 minutes

To two pounds drumettes add 2/3 cup soy sauce and 2 cups brown sugar.

Arrange drumettes on a lightly greased 9 x 13 baking dish

Bake at 300 degrees for 3 hours. Cover with foil last 1/2 hour.

Serve warm with the sauce.

CRAB ROUNDS

Baguettes Sliced 1/2" thick
1 cup mayonnaise
1/2 cup grated onion
1 cup shredded cheddar
6 drops tabasco
1/2 teaspoon curry powder
2 cans (6 1/2 ounce) crab meat
   drained

Combine all the ingredients, and put on bread toasts. Broil until golden brown.

SAUSAGE PUFFS

1 pound pork sausage
  (cook and drain fat)
1/2 cup chopped green onion
1/2 pound mushrooms chopped
3-4 cloves chopped garlic
2 eggs, lightly beaten
1/2 cup fresh bread crumbs
1 tablespoon whole mustard seed
1/2 teaspoon cayenne pepper

Cook all together, just until blended.

1 pound puff pastry
  (set at room temperature 20 minutes)
4 tablespoons melted butter

Pull puff pastry into 2 rectangles
Spread each with 1/2 sausage meat mix.
Roll up and seal seam with cold water.

Place on broiler pan with rack.
Bake at 425 degrees for 45 min.
Slice and serve.

ANCHOVY BREAD

2 cans anchovies

Make a paste of:
2 minced garlic cloves
1 teaspoon tomato paste
1 1/2 tablespoons olive oil
2 teaspoons lemon juice
black pepper
puree with the anchovies in the
  processor.

Soak the anchovies in cold water and pat dry.

Bake in a 500 degree oven.
Brown the bread on one side to toast.
Spread with anchovy mix on the other side.

Bake 10 minutes but watch closely, it may burn. Sprinkle with parsley and serve at once.

BRANDIED MUSHROOMS

1 pound mushrooms, sliced
6 tablespoons butter
1 cup dry sherry (saute until liquid is
  gone, add brandy heat and ignite.)
1/2 cup brandy
Heat 1/2 cup heavy cream and pour
  over mushrooms
dash salt

Serve on toast triangles.

BOURSIN CHEESE

3 ounces cream cheese
4 tablespoon butter
1/4 teaspoon garlic powder
2 teaspoons fresh parmesan, grated
1 tablespoon dry white wine
1 tablespoon minced parsley
dash of thyme and marjoram

Process in the food processor.

Serve with crackers.

STUFFED MUSHROOMS

1 pound hot pork sausage
1 pound large fresh mushrooms

METHOD: Remove stems-fill caps with raw sausage.

Place on ungreased sheet 350 degrees, bake for 30 minutes. May sprinkle with parmesan cheese before baking.

Garnishes:
sour cream
sliced radishes
chopped parsley
chopped red onion

POTATO BITES

1 cup light sour cream
1 green onion, chopped
2 teaspoons dijon mustard
1/4 teaspoon dried thyme

(Combine all the above and refrigerate)

METHOD: Oil a pan with olive oil

Slice 2 pounds small russet potatoes
   (1/2" thick slices)

Sprinkle with a little thyme and fresh salt and pepper.

Bake at 400 degrees - until potatoes are brown - cool slowly - top with sour cream and garnish with thyme sprig

CHICKEN WINGS

3 pounds chicken wings
1 stick butter
1 cup soy sauce
1 cup brown sugar
3/4 cup water
1/4 teaspoon dry mustard

Heat all ingredients together. Arrange in shallow dish pour sauce over wings - marinate for at least 2 hours in the fridge, and then bake at 350 for 1 1/2 hours. Serve as an appetizer.

MARINATED MUSHROOMS

2/3 cup fresh tarragon vinegar
1/2 cup salad oil
1 clove garlic crushed
1 tablespoon sugar
1 1/2 teaspoon salt
1/2 teaspoon pepper
dash of tabasco

Let these sit at room temperature for a while.

Pour over:
1/2 pound mushrooms
1 medium onion sliced thin
1/4 green pepper sliced thin

HOT BRIE APPETIZER

8" round of Brie

3 tablespoons chopped pecans
3 tablespoons brown sugar
Brandy to moisten

In a 425 degree oven, bake brie on an oven proof dish for 5-6 minutes.

Top Brie with Brandy pecan mixture.
Bake at 350 degrees for another 5 minutes or until center is soft.

Serve on hot dish with crackers.

Scotched Bacon Chestnut Appetizer

1 can drained whole water chestnuts
1 cup Scotch
1 teaspoon chopped garlic
1 teaspoon salt

Marinate the water chestnuts with the Scotch, garlic and salt for at least 24 hours. Wrap the water chestnuts in bacon (each piece cut in half crosswise will do it.) Bake the water chestnuts for about 30-45 minutes, watch that the bacon gets crisp but not burned.

Serve with a sauce made from:
1/2 cup mayonnaise
1/2 cup catsup
a little mustard and worcestershire
** sauce**
salt, pepper, and a little cayenne

Makes about 30 appetizers.

Onion Party Puffs

1 package refrigerator biscuits, cut
** in 4 pieces**

Place on cookie sheet, dot with onion butter. Bake at 400 degrees for 8 minutes.

Onion Butter

1 cup Lipton onion soup mix
1/2 pound butter

Blend well - good on baked potatoes or cooked vegetables.

GINGER SHRIMP APPETIZER

One loaf of fresh French Bread
50 large-ish fresh black shrimp
4 cloves garlic finely chopped
1 medium piece of fresh ginger
   peeled and thinly sliced

In a heavy pan brown 1/2 cube butter with sliced ginger. Take out the ginger and set aside. Put garlic into the pan and brown it and then add the shrimp and a tiny bit of water to steam the shrimp. Cover and steam on high heat for about 5 minutes or until shrimp are nicely done. Don't overcook the shrimp, they will continue to cook in the sauce. Add the ginger and serve in the pan with sliced French bread for dipping in the sauce.

PASTRY PUFFS

These are a simple appetizer. Use one package of Pepperidge Farm puff pastry dough. Cut about 2" squares and fill with a chunk of brie cheese.

Bake at 400 degrees for about 15-20 minutes. Serve hot or cold with mustard.

ARTICHOKE NIBBLES

2 jars (6 oz.) marinated artichoke
   hearts
1/2 large onion, minced
1 clove garlic, minced (the onion and
   garlic can be run through the food
   processor)
4 eggs
1/4 cup dry bread crumbs
1/4 teaspoon salt
1/8 teaspoon pepper
1/8 teaspoon oregano
1/8 teaspoon hot pepper sauce
   (tabasco)
1/2 # sharp Cheddar cheese, grated
2 tablespoons parsley, minced

Grease an 8 x 8 inch baking pan. Drain marinade from one jar of artichokes into a skillet, add onion and garlic and cook until onion is transparent. Drain second jar of artichokes, discarding marinade and chop contents of both jars. In a bowl beat eggs lightly, stir in crumbs and salt, pepper, oregano and pepper sauce. Add cheese, parsley, chopped artichokes, garlic and onion. Mix well. Pour into prepared pan and bake in 350 degree oven about 35 minutes. Remove and allow to stand for 15 minutes to set. Cut into small squares. Makes 3 to 4 dozen squares. I put this whole thing through the food processor, and this makes a quick appetizer.

SAUSAGE ROLLS

Pastry:
6 cups flour in a bowl
1 pound of lard
2 teaspoons of salt, and cut in
enough cold water to form a
dough (about 4 tablespoons)

Any good pastry will do for these. I use my grandmother's pastry recipe and freeze it. I make these into little balls and freeze them, using them later whenever I need a good pastry.

Sausage roll mixture:
Brown together 2 cloves garlic
1 pound lean sausage (hot Italian is
good or what our butcher calls
Kentucky beef sausage?)

Drain off all the fat and then add:
1/4 cup bread crumbs
a little hot sauce
green onions, finely chopped
chopped parsley

I also use this mixture for stuffed mushrooms. Roll out pastry into a rectangle. Spread with cool sausage mixture, and then roll up as a jelly roll. Cut into 2" pieces and bake until pastry is brown in a hot oven, 400 degrees, about 10 minutes.

ROASTED EGGPLANT DIP

Bake the eggplant - halved with the skin side down at 400 degrees about 40 minutes. Bake it with:

2 plum tomatoes halved
8 small onions quartered
4 large peeled garlic cloves
pinch of thyme
2 tablespoons olive oil, drizzle oil
over vegies

METHOD: peel eggplant, transfer to food processor, add thyme, pulse until smooth, then add salt and pepper. Garnish with parsley, serve at room temp.

Serve with toasted pita bread triangles.

BREADS & ROLLS

WHOLE WHEAT EGG BREAD

1/2 cup powdered milk
1 stick butter (it's best)
1/2 cup honey
2 teaspoons salt
2 packages yeast
2 eggs
4 cups whole wheat flour
3 cups unbleached regular flour

METHOD: Pour 2 cups boiling water over milk, butter, honey, and salt. Let cool to lukewarm and add yeast and eggs. Beat well. Add one cup of whole wheat flour at a time until all four are well mixed in, and then add the unbleached flour until the dough comes away from the sides of the bowl. Knead this on a lightly floured board for about 5 minutes (use unbleached flour) and let rise in a well greased bowl for about an hour until double. Form into four small loaves or two very large round loaves, and place on greased cookie sheet. Let rise 30-40 minutes and then bake at 350 for about 30 minutes for the small 40-50 minutes for the large. When I form the loaves, I put an x on top which lets me identify these in the freezer. These freeze very well.

This recipe comes to me from Judy Jenkins. Judy is a Rancher's wife and bakes up a storm all the time. This hearty whole wheat bread is a great favorite of her family and my clients.

ORANGE ROLLS

Rolls:
1 package yeast dissolved in
1/4 cup warm water
Add 1/4 cup sugar
2 eggs
1/2 cup sour cream
6 tablespoons butter
pinch salt
2 1/2 to 3 cups flour

Knead 5-10 minutes. Let rise till doubled 1-2 hours. Punch down, let rest 10 minutes. Roll out into rectangular shape. Bruch with melted butter.

Fill with the following: 1/4 cup sugar, 1 cup coconut, 2 tablespoons grated orange rind (mixed together). Place on greased 9 x 13 pan, let rise until doubled about 1 hour. Bake at 350 degrees, for 25-30 minutes.

Glaze...In saucepan, combine:
3/4 cup sugar
1/2 cup sour cream
the juice of one orange
1/4 cup butter

Boil 3 minutes, stirring, pour over warm rolls.

This recipe is from Lin Lee who runs Greystone Inn Bed and Breakfast in Livingston, Montana.

CRUMPETS

1 pint warm milk
1 teaspoon sugar
1 1/2 tablespoons dried yeast
1 ounce butter
1/4 teaspoon salt
1 pound 2 ounces flour

Scald milk, stir in sugar and add yeast when luke warm. Melt butter and add salt to the liquid. Add flour to make fairly thin batter. Cover and allow to rise for 30 minutes. Drop spoonful on greased griddle. Brown on one side, after it blisters turn over and brown the other side.

SWEET MILK DOUGHNUTS

2 tablespoons fat
1 cup sugar
1 egg
1 cup milk
4 teaspoons baking powder
1 teaspoon salt
1/2 teaspoon cinnamon
Flour to make soft dough about
    3-4 cups

Cream fat and sugar, add milk and well beaten egg, 3 cups flour sifted with dry ingredients then enough flour to make dough stiff enough to roll. Roll 1/4" thick.

Fry in deep fat 2 minutes. When cool sprinkle with powdered sugar.

When I was a girl and coming home from school, starving as usual, my grandmother had these donuts coming out hot from the fat. With a hot cocoa or cup of coffee these donuts were bliss.

BARA BRITH (WELSH BREAD)

8 ounces self rising flour
6 ounces brown sugar
6 fluid ounces cold tea
4 ounces sultanas (raisins)
4 ounces currants
1 large egg
pinch salt

Place fruit in cold tea overnight. Stir dry ingredients into fruit. Beat egg and stir in.

Bake in a well greased loaf pan for about 1 hour at 350 degrees.

GRAIN BREAD

4 cups water
1 cup Cream of the West Cereal
1 tablespoon salt
1/4 cup honey
1/4 cup molasses
Cook above for 10 min. cool to 120 degrees

Add:
1 cup flour
3 tablespoons yeast

Add:
1 egg
2 tablespoons flax seed
1 tablespoon vinegar
1/2 cup oil
1/4 cup sunflower seeds
1 tablespoon millet
8 cups flour (1/2 whole wheat)

Knead, let rise until doubled, put into loaf pans, rise.

Bake 350 degrees for 30-35 minutes. Can also use cracked wheat or rye flour.

Wonderful with a smoky cheese.

PUMPKIN BREAD

3 1/3 cups flour (sifted)
2 teaspoons soda
1 1/2 teaspoons salt
1 teaspoon cinnamon
1 teaspoon nutmeg
3 cups sugar
1 cup oil vegetable
4 eggs
2/3 cup water
1 2# can pumpkin (2 cups)

Sift dry ingredients, including sugars, into a bowl, add remaining ingredients and mix until smooth. Apportion batter into three greased and floured loaf pans.

Bake at 350 degrees for 50-60 minutes. Cool in pans, turn onto racks. Wrap and refrigerate or freeze. These freeze very well. Take out and thaw before serving.

GRAPE NUTS BREAD

1 1/2 cups grape nuts cereal
3/8 cup sugar
3 cups boiling water
3/8 cup butter
1 package yeast softened in
2 tablespoons warm water
1/2 tablespoon salt
6 cups flour

Mix grape nuts, water, sugar, butter. Pour over this mixture the 3 cups of boiling water. Let cool, stir in yeast, salt, flour. Mix well and knead well. Let rise until double. Punch down and turn out on floured board. Let rise 1/2 hour, shape into loaves. Let rise until double in size.

Bake 350 degrees for 35-40 minutes. Refrigerate or freeze, good toasted.

NORWEGIAN COFFEE RING

2 packages yeast
1 teaspoon sugar
1/4 cup warm water
1 cup scalded milk (cooled)
1/4 cup melted butter
1/3 cup sugar
1 1/2 teaspoons salt
5-6 cups flour to make a sticky dough

Mix the above together. Let rise until doubled in bulk. Roll into an 18 x 12 rectangle, spread with butter and cinnamon. Walnuts and pecans can be added. Roll up and place in a buttered bundt pan, snip top and let rise until double.

Bake for 30-40 minutes in a 350 degree oven. Drizzle with a glaze made from melted butter and powdered sugar.

LEFSE

5 cups mashed potatoes
1 teaspoon salt
1 tablespoon butter
3 cups flour

Mash the potatoes with a small amount of milk.

Mash when hot add flour when warm. Roll small balls of dough very thin and bake on a hot dry grill.

In my husband's family these are spread with whipped cream and cinnamon, rolled, sliced and eaten with the meal. I have also had them dripping with butter and honey or jam.

FLOUR TORTILLA

4 cups flour
1/3 cup lard
　(use lard, don't substitute Crisco
　etc., it doesn't turn out as well.)
1 teaspoon salt
1 cup plus of warm to hot water

Blend lard in as for pastry. Make hole in flour as for biscuits. Blend together quickly. When dough forms a ball knead briefly on a floured board. Roll out tortilla from a ball of dough the size of a golf ball. Bake on a hot, dry griddle. Put between a layer of tea towel to steam a bit. You can't buy anything vaguely like homemade tortillas, and they are easy to make.

BEST EVER ZUCCHINI BREAD

3 eggs
1 cup vegetable oil
1 1/2 cup sugar
3 medium zucchini, grated, well
   drained (2 cups)
2 teaspoons vanilla
2 cups flour
1/4 teaspoons baking powder
2 teaspoons baking soda
3 teaspoons cinnamon
1 teaspoon salt
1 cup raisins
1 cup chopped nuts (or more)

Beat eggs lightly in a large bowl. Stir in oil, sugar, vanilla, zucchini. Sift flour, baking powder, baking soda, cinnamon and salt onto wax paper. Stir into egg mixture until well blended; stir in raisins and nuts. Spoon batter into 2 well greased 8x5x3 (or standard) loaf pans.

Bake at 375 degrees for 1 hour or until done. Center springs back when lightly touched. Cool in pan on wire rack 10 min. Remove and cool completely.

This recipe comes from my friend Ruth Tarlton of Kalispell, MT.

Butterhorn Rolls

2 packages yeast softened in
1/4 cup warm water
1 tablespoon sugar

add:
1 cup scalded milk, cooled
1 cup water
6 tablespoons soft butter
1/2 cup sugar
1 teaspoon salt
3 eggs
4 cups flour, mix well and then add
about 2-3 cups more flour to make
a soft dough.

Knead lightly and set aside to rise one hour. Roll out: Spread with 1 cup butter and 1/2 cup sugar blended together. Roll out long narrow and thin, spread with 1/4 of butter mixture fold ends to center and double from one end. Repeat 4 times. Make into butterhorns, place on a greased cookie sheet, let rise until double in size, bake at 350 degrees until light brown.

Frosting

1 egg, beat until light and fluffy
1 cup powdered sugar
4 tablespoons butter
1 teaspoon vanilla

Spread on cooled butterhorns.

Banana Bread

1 1/2 cups sugar
1/2 cup margarine
add one at a time 2 eggs

Bake at 350 degrees for 1 hour in loaf pan.

Blend well and add:
1 cup mashed ripe bananas
1 teaspoon vanilla
1/2 teaspoon salt
2 cups flour

Alternately with:
1/4 cup sour milk with
1/2 teaspoon soda stirred into the
   milk

Strawberry Bread

2 cups sugar
3 cups flour
1 teaspoon each salt and soda
3 teaspoons cinnamon
1 1/4 cups oil
4 eggs
2 thawed packages of frozen
   strawberries (10 oz.)

Combine all ingredients in order and pour into 2 well greased bread pans. Bake at 350 for 1 hour, cool in the pans for 10 minutes, before inverting and then cool on a rack.

This recipe comes from Noreen Smith.

Poppyseed Bread

Ingredients:
1/2 pound butter
1 cup sugar
4 eggs (separated / beat egg whites
    to stiff peaks and retain)
1/2 pint sour cream
1 teaspoon baking soda
2 cups flour
1 tablespoon vanilla
1/3 cup poppy seeds

METHOD: Beat sugar and butter until fluffy, add egg yolks, sour cream, bakng soda, flour, vanilla and poppy seeds. Then fold in stiffly beaten egg whites. Bake in two well greased and floured 8 1/2" by 4 1/2" by 2 1/2" loaf pans. One hour at 350 degrees. Cool in pan for 1/2 hour and then put on rack to cool. Heat together until boiling and thickened: 1 stick butter, 1 cup sugar, 1 teaspoon vanilla. 1/3 cup water. Make lots of holes in the cake with a toothpick and then spoon slowly over the cake the warm not boiling hot butter sauce.

This recipe comes to me from Georgann Watson, who has owned and operated a cattle ranch in Montana most of her life.

Cinnamon Rolls

Pour 2 cups hot water in bowl, add
2 packages yeast
1/2 cup sugar
2 teaspoons salt
1/2 cup cooking oil
2 eggs

Into this mixture add
3 cups of flour beat well, then add
    about
4 more cups of flour until dough
    comes away from the bowl.

Knead for about 5 minutes, and then roll up ball and place in a greased bowl. Let rise until doubled, about 1 hour.

Roll out on floured board 1/2 of the dough into an 18 x 24 rectangle. Spread rectangle with lots of butter and cinnamon and brown sugar and walnuts. Roll up and then cut into about 2 inch pieces. Put in a heavily buttered pan and let rise for 1 hour.

Bake at 375 degrees about 30-40 minutes or until golden brown.

Russian bun variation:
Use this dough after first rising stretch a ball of dough about the size of a large egg across your hand and fill it with: cooked hamburger, cheese, cooked onion and cabbage. Bake the same as for cinnamon rolls. These freeze and travel well.

REFRIGERATOR POTATO BREAD

1 package active dry yeast
1/2 cup + 1 tablespoon sugar
1/2 cup warm water
1 cup warm milk or potato water
 (water potatoes are cooked in)
1 1/2 sticks butter (softened in warm
 water or milk)
1 tablespoon salt
2 eggs
1 cup mashed potatoes (I make these
 for dinner and use leftover
 potatoes to make this up at night)
6-7 cups flour

METHOD: Dissolve yeast and 1 tablespoon sugar in 1/2 cup warm water and proof. Add potato water, butter, 1/2 cup sugar, salt and eggs and blend. Add mashed potatoes and blend. Add flour one cup at a time for a stiff dough. Knead for 10-12 minutes. Will be smooth and elastic. Put in buttered bowl and turn over lightly to coat and refrigerate overnight. The next morning punch down and turn on floured board. Let rest 5-6 minutes. Knead 4-5 minutes without using much extra flour. Shape into 2 loaves. Put in buttered pans (use butter! the breads won't stick). Let double in the pans. This can take most of the day. Bake at 375 degrees for about an hour. Tap to see if they are done. Makes great toast.

This recipe comes to me from John Ross of Madison, Wisconsin.

Apricot Horns

Dough:
1 pound butter
1 pound creamy cottage cheese
4-5 cups flour (sometimes a little more if cottage cheese is really creamy)

Filling:
1 # dried apricots
2 cups sugar

Cook apricots until tender; drain and puree. Add sugar while still hot. Cool. Keep this in freezer or fridge and use as you like.

This is a cookie if it's small, a roll if it's large.

METHOD: Mix butter (at room temperature) with cottage cheese and flour until it forms a stiff dough. Make into 1 inch balls and store in the fridge overnight. In the morning roll each ball into a little 3 inch circle. Dip the circle in egg whites lightly beaten and then put in a teaspoon of filling. Roll outside in ground almonds.

Bake until golden brown about 15 minutes in a 375 degree oven.
Makes 11 dozen horns.

I keep the dough in fridge for as long as a month. It will get some black spots in it from the cottage cheese but they disappear when baked and they are fine. These are best made up fresh, but they can be frozen as long as they are well baked. These are really good for breakfast with strong coffee or juice.

RUSSIAN BUNS

Make a dough of the following
 ingredients:
2 packages yeast
dissolve in 2 cups warm water

add:
1/2 cup sugar
1/2 cup oil
2 teaspoons salt
2 eggs

Beat in about 4 cups of flour until you have a smooth dough, and then add 2-3 more cups to form a malleable dough. This will be quite stretchy. Knead for 5 minutes until smooth. Put in a greased bowl and let rise in a warm room for about 45 minutes. While the dough is rising brown 1 1/2 pounds ground beef (with a little onion) and salt. Let aside to cool. Grate 1/2 pound of cheddar cheese. Pinch off a ball of dough about the size of an egg and smooth in a well greased hand to form a flat piece of dough. Fill with the filling, and close the dough around the filling. Place with the pinched side down on a greased sheet. Let rise about 30 minutes and bake at 375 degrees for 15 to 20 minutes. Vegetarian buns can be made with cooked cabbage and onion in place of the meat. These pack and travel very well and freeze beautifully.

CHEESE AND MEAT BREAD

For the bread:
2 cups hot water
2 packages yeast
1/2 cup sugar
2 teaspoons salt
1/2 cup cooking oil
2 eggs
7 cups bread flour

Pour 2 cups hot water in bowl, add yeast, sugar, salt, cooking oil, and the eggs, mix together. Add 3 cups of flour and beat well, then add about 4 more cups of flour until dough comes away from the bowl. Knead for about 5 minutes, and then roll up ball and place in a greased bowl. Let rise until doubled, about 1 hour.

Roll out about 1/3 of the dough on a floured board. Make a rectangle approximately 16" x 12". Layer corned beef and swiss/cheddar/provolone cheese on the center of the rectangle. (ham, or pastrami, or other cold meats can also be used or just the cheeses.) Cut strips along the edges and braid. Follow diagram below.

Let rise on greased cookie sheet and bake at 375 degrees about 30-40 minutes or until golden brown.

To freeze, wrap in foil. This will make three large loaves.

This is an excellent picnic or backpacking bread, the dough is made from a recipe from my friend Rae Jean Fallbeck, who grew up in the Bohemian part of Nebraska. It is the easiest, most versatile dough I know. I use it for rolls, piroshkis, stuffed breads, and cinnamon rolls. Using a light hand with the flour, it makes a bread that is light as a feather, moist, and delicious.

 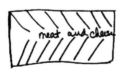

Fold strips over meat and cheese.

BREAKFAST SPECIALTIES

SWEDISH PANCAKES

(These are from My Iowa Grandmother)

**In a blender or large bowl
beat together:
4 eggs
4 tablespoons sugar
add 1 teaspoon salt
1 cup flour
2 cups milk
4 tablespoons melted butter**

METHOD: Beat in two cups milk last until well blended melt 4 tablespoons butter (do not substitute margarine) and pour this into batter beating thoroughly.

Pour into a large cast iron pancake griddle until griddle is covered thinly, and bake about a minute-flip over and bake on the other side just a little-roll up and serve with homemade syrup.

HOMEMADE SYRUP

**1 cup brown sugar
1 cup white sugar
1 cup water**

Boil about 20 minutes on a simmer until thickened

BREAKFAST SAUSAGE BAKE

When you boil potatoes for a potato salad or mashed potatoes make about 4 extra large potatoes with their skins. These potatoes are the base. In a large casserole dish grate the potatoes. Cover with sausage meat that has been cooked with a little green onion top.

Sprinkle this on the potatoes. Then mix up about 12 eggs with about 2 cups grated cheddar cheese. Pour this over the mixture and bake at 350 degrees for about 25 minutes. Mix a little tabasco in this if you like hot dishes.

Maple Bacon Oven Pancake

3 cups bisquick
2 tablespoons sugar
3 cups shredded cheddar cheese
1 1/2 cups milk
1/2 cup maple syrup
4 eggs
12 slices crisp bacon
    crumbled

Mix all together, bake in a greased 9 x 13 pan. Bake at 400 degrees for 30 minutes.

Serve with maple syrup.

This recipe is from the Yellowstone Inn Bed and Breakfast in Gardiner, Montana.

Oven Puff Pancake

Beat lightly together:
1/2 cup flour
1/2 cup milk
2 eggs lightly beaten
pinch of nutmeg

Melt a half a stick of butter in 12" skillet or glass oven dish. Bake 15-20 minutes, 425 degree oven until golden brown.

Sprinkle with 2 tablespoons powdered sugar and put back in oven briefly. Sprinkle with juice of 1/2 lemon.

Serve with jam, jelly, or marmalade.

CREAM CHEESE COFFEE CAKE

2 packages crescent rolls
2 8 ounce packages cream cheese at
    room temperature
3/4 cup sugar
1 egg (separated)
1 teaspoon vanilla

Cream cheese until smooth and fluffy. Add sugar and blend. Add egg yolk, then vanilla and blend together. Use 1 package of rolls and stretch onto a cookie sheet. Spread cream cheese filling on top of rolls. Use other package for top. Stretch them together also. Pinch sides together. Brush egg white on top. Bake at 375 degrees for 20 to 30 minutes (until brown). Glaze immediately with 1 cup powdered sugar, a little hot water and dash of vanilla. Refrigerate until chilled, then slice.

This recipe comes from Pat Cory from Tennessee.

SCOTTISH OAT SCONES

1 2/3 cups melted butter
1/3 cup milk or lite cream
1 egg
1 1/2 cups flour
1 1/4 cups quick oats
1/4 cup sugar
1 tablespoon baking powder
1 teaspoon cream of tartar
1/2 teaspoon salt

Mix all the liquids together and dump quickly over the dry ingredients. Mix very briefly and then knead lightly.

Shape dough to form 8" circle cut in wedges. Bake in a preheated hot oven, 425 degrees for 12-15 minutes.

8-12 servings

ZUCCHINI PANCAKES

4 or 5 medium zucchini
3 eggs
4 tablespoons whole wheat flour
3 tablespoons grated Parmesan
  Cheese
1 teaspoon parsley
pinch of garlic powder

Mix together lightly. And bake on a greased griddle.

Optional: lemon pepper, super salad seasonings, bacon bits, sunflower or sesame seeds, chopped mushrooms.

SOURDOUGH HOT CAKES

The night before, in glass bowl:

Mix:
1/4 cup starter
2 cups flour
1 1/2 cups water
1 teaspoon sugar

Beat well and let ferment in warm place. In morning take out 1/4 cup starter, store in refrigerator.

To remaining starter add:
1 teaspoon sugar
1/4 teaspoon salt
2 egg yolks
2 teaspoons oil

Stir well with wooden spoon. Fold in:
2 beaten egg whites
1/2 teaspoon soda dissolved in 1 tablespoon warm water. Batter will take on appearance of whipped cream.

Bake on hot griddle until bubbles appear, turn.

Serve hot with warm syrup or honey, or even better fresh Montana huckleberry jam.

PANCAKES

1 1/4 cup sifted enriched flour
1 tablespoon baking powder
1 tablespoon sugar
1/2 teaspoon salt
1 beaten egg
1 cup milk
2 tablespoons melted shortening

Sift flour with baking powder, sugar, and salt. Combine egg, milk, shortening, add to dry ingredients, stirring just until flour is moistened. Batter will be lumpy.

Bake on lightly greased griddle.

Makes 6 to 8 pancakes. Serve with homemade syrup made from 1 cup brown sugar, 1 cup white sugar and one cup water.
Boil together until thickened.

LEMON PANCAKES

3 eggs, separated
1/4 cup flour
3/4 cup cottage cheese
1/4 cup (1/2 stick) melted butter
2 tablespoons sugar
1/4 teaspoon salt
1 tablespoon grated lemon zest

Separate eggs and beat the whites until they hold stiff peaks. In another bowl, stir together remaining ingredients until well mixed. With a large spoon or spatula fold egg whites into yolk mixture. Gently stir until there are no yellow or white streaks. Heat griddle or skillet on medium heat. Grease lightly and spoon about 2-3 tablespoons batter for each cake.

Cook slowly for about 1 1/2 min. turn and cook about 30 seconds. (Rather difficult to turn.) Keep warm and serve hot. Serve with powdered sugar, raspberry syrup or any jam.

Do Ahead Bran Muffins

1/2 cup butter, melted
1 cup packed brown sugar
1/2 cup molasses
4 eggs
2 cups milk (mix together)
2 cups whole bran cereal
1 cup all purpose flour
1 cup whole wheat flour
4 teaspoons baking powder
1 teaspoon salt
1 teaspoon cinnamon
1/2 cup chopped nuts
2 tablespoons sesame seed

Mix all together lightly. Put in muffin tins about 3/4 full and then bake at 400 degrees 20-25 minutes.

Breakfast Muffins

Mix together:
1 1/2 cups flour
1/2 cup rolled oats
2 teaspoons baking powder
1 teaspoon ground cinnamon
1/2 teaspoon ginger and mace
1/4 teaspoon baking soda
1/8 teaspoon ground cloves

Add:
2 egg whites, beaten
1 cup canned pumpkin
1/2 cup light molasses
1/2 cup orange juice
1/4 cup oil
1/2 cup chopped walnuts

Bake at 375 degrees for 20-25 min.

Bran Oat Muffins

Mix together:
1 1/2 cup flour
1 cup bran cereal
1 cup rolled oats
1/2 cup brown sugar
1 1/2 teaspoons baking soda

Add:
1 1/4 cups buttermilk
1 large egg
1/4 cup butter melted

Bake at 400 degrees for 30 minutes.

Oat Bran Muffins

2 1/4 cups oat bran
1/2 cup currants
1 tablespoon brown sugar
1 teaspoon grated orange peel
1/3 cup sugar
1/2 cup orange juice
1/4 cup vegetable oil
Whites of 3 large eggs beaten stiff

Fold the whites into the bran batter.
Bake at 375 degrees for 20 minutes.

OAT BRAN APPLE MUFFINS

Mix together:
3/4 oat bran
1/2 cup whole wheat flour
1/2 cup whole bran cereal
1/4 cup packed brown sugar
2 1/2 teaspoons baking powder
1/2 teaspoon ground cinnamon
1/4 teaspoon salt

Add:
1 beaten egg
3/4 cup milk
3 tablespoons oil
1 small apple finely chopped
1/2 cup raisins

Topping:
2 tablespoons sugar
1 tablespoon flour
1 teaspoon melted butter
1/2 teaspoon ground cinnamon

Mix lightly, and bake at 400 degrees for 12-15 minutes. 12 muffins.

REFRIGERATOR BRAN MUFFINS

Mix together:
3 cups bran cereal
1 cup boiling water

Add:
1 cup vegetable oil
2 eggs
1 1/2 cups brown sugar
2 cups buttermilk
2 1/2 teaspoons baking soda
1 teaspoon salt
2 1/2 cups flour

They will keep for 6 weeks. Bake at 400 degrees for 20 minutes. Keep these in a tightly closed container in the fridge and bake as you need them.

ORANGE AND CHOCOLATE MUFFINS

1/2 cup butter
1 cup sugar
grated peel of 2 oranges
2 large eggs
1/2 cup each sour cream and orange
  juice
1 teaspoon baking powder
1/2 teaspoon soda
2 cups flour
3 ounces chocolate chopped, or mini
  semi-sweet chocolate chips

Bake at 400 degrees for 20 minutes.
Makes 10 muffins.

GINGER, LEMON AND WALNUT MUFFINS

Grated peel of 2 lemons
2 tablespoons fresh ginger, grated
1 cup sugar (put through steel blade
  in food processor)
1/2 cup sweet butter
2 eggs
1 cup sour cream or yogurt
1/2 cup chopped walnuts
1/2 teaspoon powdered ginger
1 teaspoon soda
2 cups flour

Bake at 400 degrees for 20 minutes or until
done.
Makes 12 muffins.

PINEAPPLE OATMEAL MUFFINS

8 ounce can crushed pineapple
1 cup rolled oats
1/2 cup sour cream or buttermilk
1/3 cup brown sugar
1 teaspoon grated orange peel
egg, beaten
1 1/4 cups all purpose flour
1 teaspoon baking powder
1/2 teaspoon baking soda
1 teaspoon salt

Mix all lightly together.
Bake at 400 degrees for 25 minutes.
Makes 12 large muffins.

ORANGE OATMEAL MUFFINS

Topping:
2 tablespoons brown sugar
2 teaspoons flour
1 teaspoon butter
1/4 teaspoon ground cinnamon

Muffins:
1 cup all purpose flour
1 cup quick cooking oats
1/2 cup pecans
1/4 cup sugar
2 teaspoons grated orange peel
2 teaspoons baking powder
1/2 teaspoon salt
1/2 cup orange juice
1/4 cup milk
3 tablespoons vegetable oil
1 egg, beaten

Bake at 425 degrees for 15 minutes.

Nutty Pumpkin Muffins

3/4 cups packed brown sugar
2 eggs
1/4 cup butter melted
1 cup pumpkin
1/2 cup buttermilk (beat until sugar
   dissolves)

Add:
2 cups flour
2 teaspoons baking powder
1 teaspoon each cinnamon and
   allspice
1/2 teaspoon salt
1/4 teaspoon ground cloves
1/2 cup chopped nuts

Beat just until mixed.
Bake at 400 degrees for 20 minutes.

Toasty Oat Granola

6 cups quick or old fashioned oats,
   uncooked
1/2 cup firmly packed brown sugar
3/4 cup wheat germ
1/2 cup flaked or shredded coconut
1/3 cup sesame seeds
1 cup chopped nuts
1/2 cup vegetable oil
1/3 cup honey
1 1/2 teaspoon vanilla

Heat the oil, honey, and vanilla until warm and pour over all the dry ingredients. Bake in a 350 oven for 20 minutes, stirring occasionally. I usually at least quadruple this recipe, and then freeze it after it is baked. It keeps indefinitely this way.

This recipe comes from my friend Mari Leppanen, who owned The Egg and I Gallery in Chicago.

OATMEAL MUFFINS

1 cup oatmeal
1 cup buttermilk
1 egg, beaten
1/2 cup brown sugar
1 cup whole wheat flour
1 teaspoon baking powder
1/2 teaspoon salt
1/2 teaspoon baking soda
1/3 cup oil

Combine oatmeal and buttermilk, add oil last. Stir until just moistened. Bake at 400 for 12-15 minutes. Makes 10 muffins.

SIMPLE MUFFIN MIX

8 cups flour
2 teaspoons salt
8 teaspoons baking powder
3 1/3 cups sugar

To make muffins use:
2 1/2 cups mix
1 cup milk
1 egg
1/2 cup oil

Put ingredients in a large bowl. Bake at 400 degrees for 20 minutes.

Variations: put jam in center, nuts, fruit, or 1/2 cup applesauce, add spices - 1 teaspoon cinnamon, 1/2 teaspoon nutmeg, 1/4 teaspoon allspice, add 1 cup grated zucchini and spices.

There are endless ways to vary this mix. I keep a large container of this mix in the pie cupboard in an airtight tin. Makes morning muffins very easy.

READY IN THE MORNING YEAST WAFFLES

1 package dry yeast
1/3 cup sugar
4 1/2 cups flour
3/4 teaspoon salt
2 teaspoons soda
1 quart buttermilk
1 cup melted butter

Beat by hand until batter is blended but lumpy, cover and leave overnight. In morning, separate 4 eggs; mix yolks into batter. Beat whites and fold in. Bake in waffle iron.

BEER WAFFLES

2 cups buttermilk Bisquick
1 egg
1 8 oz. can beer

Mix together and add:
1/2 cup bacon grease
1/2 cup water

The batter will be runny, but thickens up if let to sit 1/2 hour before baking in a hot greased waffle iron.

This recipe comes to me from Hallie and Amy Stephens who invite Tom and me over for brunch now and then, serving us something new and delicious each time.

Pumpkin Nut Muffins

1/2 cup shortening (butter flavored)
3/4 cup brown sugar
1/2 cup white sugar
2 large eggs
1 cup pumpkin (up to 1 1/2 cups
   can be used)
1 2/3 cup flour
1 teaspoon salt
1 teaspoon pumpkin pie spice
1/2 teaspoon cloves
1 teaspoon cinnamon
3/4 teaspoon baking powder
1/3 cup water
1/2 cup raisins
1/4 cup chopped walnuts

Mix all together and put into 12 lined muffin cups and bake 350 degrees for 20-25 minutes.

Giant Muffin Mix

(Very large recipe)

Pour 2 cups boiling water over 4 cups all-bran cereal and 2 cups shredded wheat cereal. Let cool. Cream together 3 cups sugar and 1 heaping cup shortening. Add four eggs. Beat well and stir in 1 quart buttermilk. Stir cooled cereal mixture into batter. Add 5 cups flour, 5 tablespoons baking powder, and 1 teaspoon salt.

NOTE: Fold in dry ingredients until just barely moistened. DO NOT OVERMIX!!! Spoon into paper liners in muffin pans and bake in 425 degree oven for 20 minutes. Sprinkle cinnamon sugar on these if you like. Add nuts and raisins if you like. This batter will keep completely mixed in the fridge for about a month. Bake as you want them, but they are actually best after they have been in the fridge for a few days. Keep in an airtight container.

CAKES & COOKIES

MEE'S CAKE

Separate 7 eggs, beat whites until
   very stiff.

Cream together:
1 1/2 cups margarine
3 cups sugar
2 teaspoons vanilla
7 egg yolks

Add:
3 cups flour
1/4 teaspoon soda

Add: 1 cup sour cream
Fold in egg whites

Bake at 350 degrees for 30-40 minutes.

Sprinkle with powdered sugar when cool.

A 9 x 13 pan should be used, or make 3 layers and spread raspberry jam in between the layers.

This recipe comes to me from Judy Jenkins, of Wilsall, MT.

BUTTERFLY CAKES

8 ounces self-raising flour
8 ounces sugar
8 ounces margarine
3 eggs

Beat these together, add eggs, and then fold in flour.

Bake in paper cup in a muffin tin at 375 degrees for 15-20 minutes.

Cut a hole in the top. Make a butter icing of powdered sugar, butter and cream, fill the hole with icing and then cut the piece that was taken from the top in two pieces and insert them as wings.

This recipe was given to me by Ivy Davies, Tufton, Pembrokeshire Wales. Children love it.

COCA COLA CAKE

2 cups flour
2 sticks margarine
1 cup coke
1/2 cup Buttermilk
2 beaten eggs
1 teaspoon vanilla
1/2 teaspoon salt
3 tablespoons cocoa
1 teaspoon soda
2 cups sugar

Sift together dry ingredients, bring margarine, cocoa, to a boil, pour over dry ingredients. Mix and add remaining ingredients, beat well and pour into ungreased
9 x 13 pyrex dish. Bake 30-35 minutes at 350 degrees.

This recipe was sent to me by Sherri Tullos, of Louisiana.

ICING

1 stick margarine
3 tablespoons cocoa
7 tablespoons coke
1 cup chopped pecans or walnuts
1 box confectioner's sugar

Bring margarine, coke, and cocoa to a boil, pour over a box of confectioner's sugar and add chopped nuts, spread over cooled cake.

CREAM SHERRY BUNDT CAKE

1 package yellow cake mix
1 package instant vanilla pudding mix
4 eggs
3/4 oil
3/4 cup sherry
1 teaspoon nutmeg

Beat all together for 4 minutes, put into well buttered Bundt pan. Bake at 350 degrees for 50 minutes. Sift powdered sugar over top or glaze. Delicious with tea.

This recipe comes from Sherra Walker.

Chocolate Mayonnaise Cake

1 1/2 cups sugar
1 cup mayonnaise
2 teaspoons vanilla
2 cups flour
5 teaspoons cocoa
2 teaspoons soda
1 cup warm water

Beat all together with electric mixer until very smooth. Pour into a 9 x 13 pan or Bundt pan. Bake at 350 degrees for 30 minutes or longer.

Noreen's Chocolate Chip Icing

1/2 cup butter
2 eggs
1 cup melted chocolate chips

Beat ingredients together. Simple and delicious. Put in fridge for a little to firm up. I double this to frost my 3 layer chocolate mayo cake.

Butter Egg Frosting

1 egg, beaten well
1 pound powdered sugar
1/2 cup butter
2 tablespoons cream
1 teaspoon vanilla or rum

Beat with electric mixer until perfectly smooth.

BLACK BOTTOM CUPCAKES

Cake:
3 cups flour
1/2 cup cocoa
2 cups sugar
1 teaspoon salt
2 teaspoons soda
pour in 2 cups water
2 tablespoons vinegar
2/3 cup oil
2 teaspoons vanilla

Filling:
8 ounces cream cheese
1 egg
1/3 cup sugar
6 ounces chocolate chips
mix well

METHOD: Mix all ingredients for cake together and put into muffin cups. Slip one teaspoon of filling into each cake. Bake at 350 degrees for 20 minutes. These need no frosting. Older kids love these.

On one of our June trips, Margaret Martin, of Boise, Idaho taught us how to Wang-Ho for these cupcakes, when you are down to one cupcake and you have to vie for it, use WANG HO!!!!!!!!!!!!!! It goes like this: Knock three times on your knee, and on the third knock put out any number of fingers on the hand. The self-appointed captain, (there's always one of these) then counts the fingers out, and counts around the circle. The last person who is counted wins the cupcake, brownie, apricot bar, or whatever you've got. Any questions? Give us a call. This should be fun to explain on the phone.

This recipe is from Ellie Raffety and the Catholic women of Anaconda, Montana.

GRANDMA'S SPECIAL-TEA COOKIES

Sift together:
2 1/4 cups sifted flour
1/2 teaspoon salt and
1 cup sifted confectioner's sugar into
   large bowl

Cut in:
1 cup soft butter until mixture
   resembles coarse meal

Beat:
1 egg until light = 4 tablespoons

Sprinkle:
2 tablespoons of the beaten egg and
2 teaspoons vanilla over mixture;
   blend well and form into a ball.
   Dough may be chilled if desired.

Roll out on floured pastry cloth or board (one-third at a time) to 1/8" thickness.
Cut into desired shapes with cookie cutter or pastry wheel. Place on ungreased baking sheets. Brush with remaining beaten egg.

Bake at 400 degrees for 5 to 7 min.
Makes about 5 dozen.

If you have been looking for a classic Christmas cookie dough to roll out, this is it! It is easy to handle, makes very thin cookies, and can be decorated with icings and will stay crisp and keep its shape.

CHOCOLATE SQUARES

Ungreased 8" x 8" pan.

Bottom layer:
1/2 cup butter
1/4 cup white sugar
1 egg
4 rounded tablespoons cocoa
1 teaspoon vanilla
2 cups graham crumbs
1 cup shredded coconut
1/2 cup chopped nuts

Mix and press into pan.

Second layer:
1/4 cup melted butter
2 tablespoons custard powder
  (Bird's)
2 scant cups icing sugar
Mix with just enough milk so it will
  spread.

Spread layer 2 over layer 1.
Let chill 20 min.

Icing:
Melt together 2 squares unsweetened chocolate and 1 square semi-sweet (or 3 oz. whatever you have on hand). Spread on top.

DEVILS FOOD CAKE

1/4 cup shortening

2 eggs

1 cup sugar

1 1/2 cups sifted flour

2 squares bitter chocolate
  (unsweetened)

1 1/2 teaspoons baking powder

1/2 teaspoon salt

1/2 cup thick sour milk or buttermilk

1/2 cup boiling water

1 teaspoon soda

1 teaspoon vanilla

Mix all in order.

Bake in a 9 x 13 pan at 350 degrees for 30 minutes.

CHOCOLATE FROSTING

Put in pan:

1 cup sugar

2 tablespoons butter

3 tablespoons milk

2 tablespoons cocoa

1 egg, beaten

Put over fire and let come to a good rolling boil, stirring all the time. Remove from heat and beat until thick enough to spread on cake.

CHOCOLATE RASPBERRY CAKE

3/4 cup cake flour
1 cup sugar
1/2 cup unsweetened
   Dutch processed cocoa powder
1/4 teaspoon salt
1/4 teaspoon baking powder
8 eggs, separated
1/3 cup vegetable oil
1 teaspoon vanilla
1 cup seedless raspberry jam
Chocolate Whipped Cream Frosting
   (at the end)

1. Preheat the oven to moderate (350 degrees). Grease three 9 inch round cake pans. Line bottoms with waxed paper circles. Dust the sides with flour; tap out the excess.

2. Stir together 3/4 cup cake flour, 1/4 cup sugar, cocoa powder, salt, and baking powder in a medium sized bowl.

3. Beat together egg yolk, 1/2 cup sugar and oil in large bowl until thick and pale yellow. Beat in the vanilla.

4. Beat egg whites with clean beaters in medium bowl until foamy. Gradually add the remaining 1/4 cup sugar, 1 tablespoon at a time, beating until stiff, but not dry, peaks form.

5. Sift 1/3 of the flour mixture over the egg yolk mixture and add 1/3 of egg whites. Gently fold until combined. Repeat with remaining flour mixture and egg white mixture in 2 more additions. Divide batter equally among the three pans.

6. Bake in preheated moderate oven for 15 to 18 minutes or until a toothpick inserted in centers comes out clean. Loosen sides of pan with a thin knife. Immediately invert cakes onto wire racks to cool completely. Remove waxed paper.

7. Place one cake layer on serving plate. Spread top with half the jam. Spread about 2/3 cup of frosting over the raspberry jam. Stack the second layer on top of first. Spread with remaining jam and about 2/3 cup of frosting. Place third on top. Frost top and sides with remaining frosting.

Refrigerate. Makes 12 servings.

HAP'S NEW CHEESECAKE

(no water bath)

1-3 tablespoons butter
4-6 graham crackers, crushed
5 (8 ounce) packages cream cheese
1 3/4 cups sugar
3 tablespoons flour
5 eggs plus 2 egg yolks (or 6 eggs)
1/4 cup cream
1 lemon (juice and grated rind)
1 teaspoon vanilla

Have all ingredients at room temperature. Preheat oven to 475 degrees. Grease a 9 or 10 inch springform pan. Coat sides and bottom of pan with crumbs, shake out excess. In electric mixer, large bowl, medium high speed, beat cream cheese until fluffy. Add sugar and flour, a little at a time, beat well after each addition. Add eggs, 1 at a time, beat well after each. Beat in vanilla, lemon juice and rind. Turn beater to high, beat 1 minute longer. Bake at 475 degrees for 15 min. Reduce heat to 200 degrees, bake 1 hour. Turn off oven, let cake cool in oven 1 hour. Remove from oven and cool on rack for 1 more hour. Loosen sides with a spatula. Invert onto serving platter. Cover loosely, refrigerate at least 1 hour before serving. Keep leftover cake refrigerated, covered. Can be frozen.

Hap Reubens is one of Livingston's great cooks.

CHOCOLATE WHIPPED CREAM FROSTING

3 squares semi-sweet chocolate
2 tablespoons unsalted butter
1/3 cup plus 1 1/4 cups heavy cream
2 tablespoons confectioner's sugar
1 teaspoon vanilla

1. Melt together chocolate, butter and 1/3 cup heavy cream in top of a double boiler over hot, not boiling water; stir until smooth. Cool completely.

2. Beat together the remaining 1 1/4 cups heavy cream, confectioner's sugar and vanilla in medium sized bowl just until soft peaks begin to form. Do not over-beat or frosting will become grainy.

3. Fold 1/3 of the whipped cream into the chocolate mixture just until combined. Fold the chocolate mixture into the remaining whipped cream just until combined.

Makes about three cups. Enough to fill and frost three 9 inch layer cakes.

Rhubarb Cake

1 1/2 cups brown sugar
1/2 cup butter
2 1/2 cups flour
1 teaspoon soda
1 teaspoon salt
1 cup sour milk
1 teaspoon vanilla
1 1/2 cups raw chopped rhubarb

Mix together in order and bake in an 8" x 8" glass cake pan. Bake at 350 degrees for 45 minutes. Sprinkle with 1/2 cup white sugar and 1 teaspoon cinnamon before baking.

IOWA DUMP CAKE

1 can pie filling
1 cup crushed pineapple, undrained
1 package white or yellow cake mix
1/2 cup nuts
1 stick butter

Grease and flour a 9" x 13" glass cake pan.

Drizzle with butter and bake at 350 degrees for 1 hour.

FRYSTEKAKE
PRESIDENT'S CAKE

1 egg yolk
2 tablespoons cream
2/3 cup sugar
2 cups flour
1 teaspoon baking powder
1/2 cup margarine
3 tablespoons margarine

Mix all together. Take 2/3 of dough and spread on bottom and sides of 9" x 13" pan.

Filling:
1/2 cup almond paste
1 1/2 cups powdered sugar
3 egg whites

Mix all together and pour in over crust. Take remainder of dough, roll out and cut in strips. Make lattice on top of filling. Bake in a 350 degree oven, until golden brown.

This recipe comes from Tom's sister, Kathy Murphy. Wonderful with coffee in the snow!

BETTER THAN ROBERT REDFORD CAKE

1 1/2 cups flour
1 1/2 sticks margarine
1 1/2 cups chopped nuts
1 8 ounce package softened cream cheese
1 cup powdered sugar
2 small containers whipped topping
2 packages of instant chocolate pudding
3 1/2 cups milk
nuts for garnish

Mix flour and margarine to coarse crumbs. Add nuts and press into a 9 x 13 pan. Bake at 400 degrees for 20 minutes and cool. Blend cream cheese and sugar and fold in one container whipped topping. Spread this on bottom layer in pan. Beat pudding mixes with milk and spread over cheese layer. Cover with remaining whipped topping and sprinkle with nuts. Chill up to overnight and cut into squares to serve.

Linda Brehm of Livingston gave me this recipe - when Robert Redford was doing "A River Runs Through It" - in our town.

TRIPLE CHOCOLATE CAKE

1 package (2 layer size) chocolate cake mix
1 package (4 serving size) chocolate instant pudding
2 eggs
1 1/3 cups milk
1 package chocolate chips (12 ounce)

Mix all in a bowl (don't over mix). Bake 50-55 minutes in a greased and floured bundt pan. Cool 15 minutes in pan. Serve with whipped cream or ice cream. Can be frozen and served at a later time.

This recipe was given to me by Dorothy Codling of California as a result of our discussions about the best chocolate recipes in the world.

Hundred Dollar Cake

3 cups flour
1 1/2 cups sugar
2 1/4 teaspoons baking powder
2 1/4 teaspoons soda
6 tablespoons cocoa
1 1/2 cups water
1 1/2 cups salad dressing (store
  brand el cheapo is best)
3 teaspoons vanilla

Dump all in a large bowl and mix well with a beater. Portion into 3-9" pans that are well greased and lined with waxed paper, greased and floured again. Bake at 350 degrees for about 25 minutes. Let cool 15 minutes in pan and then invert on waxed paper or a rack.

Icing:
2 sticks butter (don't substitute soft
  margarine)
2 egg yolks
1 12 oz. package chocolate chips
  melted
2 teaspoons vanilla

Beat on high speed of electric mixer until smooth and blended, set in fridge to firm up until the cake is completely cool. Ice when cake is cool and store in fridge.
Serves 12.

Apple Torte

3 egg whites
1 cup white sugar
1/4 cup brown sugar
1/2 cup flour
1 teaspoon baking powder
1/2 teaspoon salt
2 medium tart apples chopped fine
    (I used granny smith)
1 cup chopped nuts
2 teaspoons mixed spices - apple pie
    spice, cinnamon, cloves, nutmeg
whipped cream

Beat egg whites until stiff. Add sugar gradually, continuing to beat. Fold in dry ingredients. Add finely chopped apples and nuts. Pour into a buttered 10 inch pie pan. Bake about 45 minutes at 375 degrees. Serve with ice cream or whipped cream.

Chocolate Zucchini Cake

1/2 cup margarine
1/2 cup oil
1 3/4 cup sugar
2 eggs
1/2 cup sour milk
2 1/2 cups flour
4 tablespoons cocoa
1/2 teaspoon baking powder
1 teaspoon soda
1/2 teaspoon cinnamon
1/2 teaspoon cloves
2 cups finely chopped zucchini

Beat all together, chocolate chips on top, bake at 325 degrees for 35 minutes.

Glaze:
3 tablespoons butter
3 tablespoons cocoa
1 cup powdered sugar
1 teaspoon vanilla
1 teaspoon hot water

Blend together and drizzle over the cake.

Gooey Butter Cake

1 yellow cake mix
1 egg
1 stick butter
(Mix together with fingers, put into 9 x 13 pan)

1 pound box (3 1/2 cups) powdered
   sugar
8 ounces cream cheese
2 eggs
1/2 teaspoon vanilla

(Beat together pour over cake) Sprinkle with almonds. Bake 350 for 35 minutes or until golden - sprinkle with powdered sugar when cool.

Old English Fruit Cake

1 1/2 cups mixed light and dark raisins
1 cup currants
2/4 cup sliced dates
1 pound mixed glace fruits
1/2 cup glace cherries, halved
1 pound walnuts chopped coarsely
2 1/2 cups flour
1/2 teaspoon each soda and salt
1/2 teaspoon each cinnamon, ginger
1/2 teaspoon each cloves and mace
1 cup butter
1 cup brown sugar
4 eggs
1/2 cup currant jelly
1/4 cup molasses
1 tablespoon brandy

Heat oven to 250 degrees. Grease two 8 x 4 - 3 loaf pans; line with 2 layers of heavy brown paper, then with 2 layers of waxed paper, greasing each layer. (Cut paper to fit pans and extend 3/4" above tops.) Rinse raisins and currants with hot water, drain and mix with dates, glace fruits, and walnuts. Sift flour with soda, salt, and spices over the fruit mixture, mix well. In another bowl cream butter with sugar until fluffy. Beat in eggs 1 at a time, then jelly molasses, and brandy. Pour over the first mixture and stir until well blended. Pour into lined pans. Bake 3 to 3 1/2 hours, or until no mark is left when top is touched lightly with a finger. To prevent browning and drying of tops, lay a piece of foil, over pans for the last 1/2 hour. Let cool in the pans, then turn out, remove paper and wrap in foil, or waxed paper; store in refrigerator. (If you wish, unwrap cake occasionally and drizzle a little fruit juice, cider, or sherry or brandy over it, then rewrap and refrigerate.)

This was our traditional Christmas cake. It came, I believe, from an old Diamond Walnut cookbook.

CHOCOLATE UPSIDE DOWN CAKE

ALSO KNOWN AS PASSION CHOCOLATE CAKE

1 cup flour
3/4 cup sugar
1/2 teaspoon salt
2 teaspoons baking powder
2 tablespoons cocoa
2 tablespoons butter
1/2 cup milk
1 teaspoon vanilla

Beat well pour in greased 8" x 8" glass dish.

Mix and spread the following over top:
1/2 cup white sugar
1/2 cup brown sugar
2 tablespoons cocoa
1 cup hot water

Bake at 350 degrees for 30 minutes. Serve with fresh cream.

This recipe comes from Oasa Murphy, Tom's mother. The reason we call this cake Passion Cake is that one time when Tom and I lived in the Black Hills we had a terrible three day blizzard, and we had run out of cocoa, and Tom walked to the grocery store to get it so we could make this cake. As he walked out into the storm and disappeared after about 1 minute, I thought "This guy really has a passion for chocolate." We renamed the cake when he got home.

CARROT CAKE

2 cups flour
2 cups sugar
2 teaspoons soda
1 teaspoon salt
1 teaspoon nutmeg
2 teaspoons cinnamon
1 teaspoon cloves
1 cup Wesson oil
4 eggs
3 cups carrots, shredded
1 cup chopped pineapple
1 cup raisins
nutmeats

Mix all together. Put in a 9 x 13 pan, well greased. Bake at 350 degrees for 35-40 minutes.

Cream Cheese Frosting:
8 ounces of cream cheese
4 ounces butter
3-4 cups of powdered sugar
1 tablespoon vanilla

Cream to frosting consistency. Beat in an electric mixer until silky.

This recipe comes from Lavonne Howard of Livingston, MT.

CHOCOLATE PRALINE CAKE

Cake:
1/2 cup butter or margarine
1/4 cup whipping cream
1 cup packed brown sugar
3/4 cup coarsely chopped pecans
1 package Devils Food Cake Mix
1 1/4 cups water
1/3 cup oil
3 eggs

In a small heavy saucepan: combine butter, whipping cream, and brown sugar; heat over low heat until butter is melted, stirring occasionally. Pour into two 9 or 8 inch round cake pans - sprinkle evenly with chopped pecans. In large bowl, combine cake mix, water, oil and eggs at low speed until moistened, beat two minutes on high speed. Carefully spoon batter over pecan mixture. Bake at 325 degrees for 35-45 min. Cool 5 min. Remove from pans, cool completely.

Topping:
1/3 cup whipping cream
1/4 cup powdered sugar
1/4 teaspoon vanilla
whole pecans if desired
chocolate curls, if desired

In small bowl beat whipping cream until soft peaks form. Blend in powdered sugar and vanilla, beat until stiff peaks form. Place one layer on serving plate, on the side up spread with 1/2 whipping cream. Top with second layer. Top with whipping cream. Garnish with pecans and chocolate curls. Store in refrigerator.

This recipe comes from Margaret Martin of Boise, ID.

Banana Bars

1 medium banana, mashed
1 1/2 cups shortening
2 eggs
1 1/2 cups flour
1 cup sugar
1/2 teaspoon soda
1/2 teaspoon salt
1/3 cup milk
Add 1 teaspoon lemon juice to milk
   to sour it
Add nuts if desired

Mix all together in order given. Put in a 9 x 13 pan (greased and floured).

Bake at 350 degrees for 25 to 30 minutes.

Frosting

2 tablespoons butter
2 cups powdered sugar
1/2 teaspoon salt
1 teaspoon vanilla
1/2 medium, banana well mashed

Beat until smooth and creamy.

Frost on cooled bars.

Apricot Nuggets

1 pound powdered sugar
6 tablespoons melted butter or
   margarine
2 tablespoons orange juice
1/2 teaspoon vanilla
1 - 11 ounce package dried apricots
   ground or chopped fine.

Combine first 4 ingredients. Add apricots and knead until well mixed. Roll into 1" balls and roll in chopped nuts or coconut. Store in covered container in refrigerator or freeze. These improve with age. Makes 40. Can double recipe.

This recipe comes to me from Don Walters' wife, Clarice, of Bozeman, MT.

CHEWY PECAN COOKIES

2 sticks of butter
1 box of brown sugar
2 eggs beaten
2 1/2 cups of flour
1/2 teaspoon of soda
1 teaspoon of vanilla
1 cup of nuts

Drop by teaspoonful and bake on a greased cookie sheet. Bake 12 minutes at 325 degrees.

Store these in a cookie tin with a slice of bread to keep them chewy.

This recipe comes to me from Evelyn Parker.

CHOCOLATE MOUNTAIN BARS

1/2 cup margarine
1/2 cup cocoa
2 cup sugar
1/2 cup milk
1/4 teaspoon salt
(Boil together, butter, cocoa, sugar,
  salt and milk for 2 minutes,
  stirring constantly.)

Remove from heat and add:
3 cups uncooked oatmeal
1/2 cup peanut butter
1/2 cup nuts
1/2 cup coconut
1 teaspoon vanilla

1. Pour into buttered 9" pan, chill several hours.

2. Scoop by tablespoon onto wax paper. The size depends on how much you scoop. Chill for several hours.

This recipe comes from Betty Hoge of Seattle, WA.

MONTANA COWBOY COOKIES

Mix:
1 cup margarine
1 cup oil
1 cup white sugar
1 cup brown sugar
1 egg

Add:
3 1/2 cups flour
1 teaspoon soda
1 teaspoon cream of tartar
1/2 teaspoon salt
1 teaspoon vanilla

Add:
1 cup rice krispies
1 cup oatmeal

Bake by rounded tablespoons full at 350 degrees for about 8-12 minutes.

MONSTER COOKIES

Method: Read this carefully before you begin.

Use a very large bowl

2 pounds brown sugar
4 cups white sugar (can decrease this a little)
1 tablespoon vanilla
8 teaspoons soda
1 tablespoon Karo syrup
1 pound margarine (not soft type)
2.8 pound jar peanut butter
18 cups quick oatmeal
2 12 oz. packages chocolate chips
1 dozen eggs
2 cups walnuts or pecans coarsely chopped

other options
Bag of M&M's (but these don't keep as well)
1 box of raisins

Mix together sugars, margarine and eggs with electric beater or by hand until thoroughly mixed. Add peanut butter, vanilla, and syrup. When that is thoroughly mixed add oatmeal, nuts and chips. There is no flour in this dough, and it is sticky. Form into patties about 3 inches across and 1/2 inch thick. Place cookies on a well greased cookie sheet (4 large cookies fit on one large cookie sheet.) Bake at 350 for about 15 minutes. They will look puffy and like they aren't quite well done, but they are best this way. Leave them on the cookie sheet until they firm up and then dry on racks until cool.

As you will notice this is a huge batch, but these keep very well in the freezer unbaked for ages. So here's what you do, divide the dough into about 8 sections and put it in Tupperware or plastic bags and just get it out the night before when you need a batch. Bake like fresh dough in the morning.

These are considered survival food in Montana. A couple of these in your pack and you can go all day.

This recipe was taken from our local paper, The Livingston Enterprise.

SUGAR COOKIES

1 cup powdered sugar
1 cup butter
1 egg
2 cups flour
2 teaspoons vanilla
1/2 teaspoon cream of tartar

Blend powdered sugar and butter until silky, add the egg, and beat again. Add the dry ingredients and blend well. Place a tablespoon of dough on a greased cookie sheet and flatten with a glass dipped in granulated sugar. Bake at 400 degrees for about 6-8 minutes or until the edges brown.

These are the lightest sugar cookies imaginable, and, of course, the recipe came from my grandmother Griffith.

BEST ZUCCHINI BARS

Bars:
2 cups sugar
1 cup oil
3 eggs
2 cups flour
1 teaspoon cinnamon
1 teaspoon salt
3/4 cup rolled oats
2 teaspoons baking soda
1/4 teaspoon baking powder
1 teaspoon vanilla
2 cups shredded zucchini
1 small carrot, shredded
1 cup nuts

Beat together sugar, oil, and eggs in large bowl. Beat in flour, cinnamon, salt, baking soda, baking powder, and vanilla. Beat 1-2 minutes until well mixed. Fold in zucchini, carrot, oats, and nuts. Bake in a jelly roll pan at 350 degrees for 15-20 min.

Frosting:
1/2 cup soft butter
1/4 teaspoon almond extract
2 teaspoons vanilla
2 1/2 cups confectioners sugar
1-3 ounce package soft cream
   cheese

Tom's sister Ginny Waterland gave me this recipe.

CHOCOLATE CASHEW TOFFEE

1 1/4 cup packed brown sugar
1/4 cup light corn syrup
5 tablespoons unsalted butter, cut in
  bits
1 tablespoon cider vinegar
1 tablespoon vanilla
1 cup chocolate chips
2 tablespoons coarsely grated
  paraffin
3/4 cup roasted salted cashews

In a heavy 2 quart saucepan combine brown sugar, corn syrup, butter, vinegar, and 1/4 cup water, boil over moderate heat stirring down sugar crystal until 290 degrees on the candy thermometer, stir in vanilla and pour into a buttered 13" x 9" pan tilting and spreading mixture.

Melt over simmering water chocolate bits and paraffin and spread it over warm but not scalding hot toffee.

Then sprinkle with cashews, chill 30 minutes. Lift out whole and chop into serving pieces.

Store in waxed paper in air tight container.

FROSTED CREAMS

1 cup shortening
1/2 cup sugar
1/2 molasses
1 teaspoon cloves
1 teaspoon cinnamon
1 teaspoon allspice
1 teaspoon ginger
2 eggs
1/2 cup sour milk
1 teaspoon soda
2 cups flour

Mix all together, dissolve soda in milk before adding. Bake on a greased cookie sheet about 2 tablespoons of dough to a cookie. Frost with a white or chocolate frosting made of powdered sugar, butter, vanilla and a little cream. Frost while still warm so the frosting glazes.

These cookies are part of one of my earliest memories of a visit to my Auntie Pearl's house. I was given a huge glass of milk and a plate of these cookies. To be polite I ate the whole plateful, and got a severe scolding from my mother on the walk home.

CREAM CHEESE BARS

1/3 cup butter
1/3 cup brown sugar
1 cup sifted flour
1/2 cup chopped walnuts
1/4 cup sugar
1 8 oz. package cream cheese, softened
1 egg, beaten
2 tablespoons milk
1 tablespoon lemon juice
1/2 tablespoon vanilla

Cream butter and brown sugar until light and fluffy. Add flour and walnuts. Cream until mixture forms crumbs. Set aside one cup of mixture for topping. Press remaining crumbs into ungreased 8" x 8" square pan. Bake in 350 degrees oven for 12-15 min. Cool. Combine white sugar and cream cheese and beat until smooth. Add egg, milk, lemon juice, and vanilla and beat thoroughly. Spread evenly over baked crumbs; sprinkle remaining 1 cup crumbs over cream cheese mixture. Bake at 350 degrees for 25-30 min. Cut into 2" x 1" bars.

This recipe comes to me from Ginny Waterland, Tom's sister.

CARROT BARS

4 eggs
2 cups of sugar
3/4 cup oil
2 cups flour
2 teaspoons soda
1 teaspoon of salt
2 teaspoons cinnamon
1 1/2 cups cooked carrots, mashed

Beat eggs and add remaining ingredients. Put in 9 x 13 greased pan. Bake at 350 degrees for 30 minutes. Cool.

FROSTING

4 teaspoons soft margarine
16 ounces cream cheese
1 pound powder sugar
2 teaspoons vanilla

Cream ingredients together, use for frosting carrot bars, when cool.

NUT GOODIE BARS
READ WHOLE RECIPE BEFORE STARTING

Layer #1

1 12 oz. pkg. Hershey's Semi-Sweet Chocolate Chips
1 12 oz. pkg. Tollhouse Butterscotch Chips
2 cups peanut butter (Jif Creamy)

Note: Put into bowl and melt in microwave about 3 1/2 min. on med. low. Stir in between. Sets really nice.
(Note: I do above in microwave) This totals 4 cups, 1/2 of microwave is 2 cups measuring cup full.

OR: Melt above together in double boiler. Will be 1/2. Put half in greased pan. (Jelly Roll Size Pan) Grease Jelly Roll Pan with either butter or margarine, NOT LARD. Set rest aside for later use, put Jelly Roll Pan in freezer so it gets really cold.

Layer #2
Mix together: (use Large Mixing Bowl)
1/2 cup evaporated milk
1 cup butter (use butter)
1/4 cup dry vanilla pudding mix (not instant)
melt in small bowl in microwave, med. low approx. 4 min. stir in between.
Boil 1 min. or heat (Don't boil or heat very long or until it looks curdled.)

Take off heat or out of microwave and add:
2 pounds powdered sugar
1 1/2 to 2 tsp. vanilla (white vanilla if possible)

Mix with electric mixer until creamy. Pour over layer 1.

Layer #3
Add 2 to 3 cups (2 1/2 cups) of Spanish Peanuts (Don't use Raw Spanish Peanuts) to rest of chocolate-butterscotch mixture and spread over Layer 2.

Keep in refrigerator or freezer. Cut before they get completely set. After cut, then put back into freezer and freeze until solid. Approx. 4-5 hours. Then put into another container.

NOTE: No Need To Put Into Freezer After Layer 2 (White Mixture) As It Should Be Thick Enough.

This recipe comes from Bonnie Zastrow from North Dakota.

Sour Cream Chocolate Chip Cookies

1/2 cup white sugar
1 cup brown sugar
2 cups sour cream
   (Not commercial sour cream, but
   whipping cream soured with
   1 tablespoon vinegar per cup)
2 eggs
2 teaspoons baking powder
1 teaspoon soda
1 teaspoon vanilla
12 ounces chocolate chips

Flour to right consistency (3-4 cups) This
will be a stiff batter.

Bake at 375 degrees on a greased cookie
sheet.

Birds Nests

1/4 cup brown sugar
1/2 cup butter (cream together)

Add:
1 egg yolk (beaten well)
1 cup flour

Form in balls, dip in slightly beaten egg
white. Put on well greased cookie sheet,
make a thumbprint hole in each cookie.

Bake 8 minutes. Punch hole again. Bake
another 10 minutes or until golden brown.
Remove from oven and when they are cool
fill with raspberry jam.

I usually at least quadruple this recipe.

OVERNIGHT COOKIE

Blend:
1 1/2 cups margarine, at room
   temperature
1 cup white sugar
1 cup brown sugar

Add:
3 eggs, beating after each
4 cups flour
1/2 teaspoon salt
2 teaspoons soda
1 teaspoon cinnamon
1/2 teaspoon nutmeg
1/2 teaspoon cloves
1/4 teaspoon allspice
1 cup chopped nuts

Press into 9 x 13 or 7 1/2 x 12 pan. Cover with plastic, put in refrigerator overnight. To bake cut pan of dough in 3rd's, take out 1/2 of one section, slice thin with a sharp knife. Bake at 375 degrees for 5 min. 8-10 dozen.

ISRAELI BROWNIES

1 package (8 squares) unsweetened
   chocolate (Yes, it's true!)
1 cup butter
5 eggs
2 1/2 cups sugar
2 teaspoons vanilla
1 1/2 cups flour
2 cups coarsely chopped walnuts

METHOD: Melt chocolate with butter over very low heat. Cool. Beat eggs, sugar, vanilla in large mixer bowl until very smooth. Blend in slightly cooled chocolate mixture, and then nuts. Spread in 9 x 13 pan. Bake at 375 degrees for 35-45 minutes. It will seem like they aren't really done and even the old toothpick in the center routine won't work for these. Just take them out and let them set until cool before you cut them into pieces.

CHOCOLATE NUT LOGS
ALSO CALLED ANTELOPE TOES

3/4 cup butter or margarine
3/4 cup sugar
1 teaspoon vanilla extract
1 egg
2 cups flour
1/2 teaspoon salt
1 pkg. semisweet chocolate chips-
  preferably mini size
1 teaspoon shortening
finely chopped nuts or sprinkles

Baking time 12-15 minutes per sheet in a 350 degree oven.

Step 1: Cream butter, sugar, vanilla and egg until light.
Step 2: Mix flour & salt, add to first mix. Mix until well blended.
Step 3: Stir in 1/2 cup of mini chips.
Step 4: Use one tsp. per cookie, shape into log, arrange on an ungreased cookie sheet.
Step 5: Bake and cool on wire racks
Step 6: Melt 1/2 12 oz. package chocolate chips with shortening.

When cookies are cool, dip 1/2 into melted chocolate. Sprinkle with nuts or sprinkles. Let stand on waxed paper until firm. We actually like these better without the nuts. This recipe is easily doubled or tripled and put in the freezer baked or raw. If you triple it you will always have them, even in the middle of the night.

This recipe comes to me from David Offenbach of New York.

BUTTERCREAMS FOR CHRISTMAS

Crust:
Mix together in a bowl -
1 cup margarine
1 cup powdered sugar
1 teaspoon salt
2 teaspoons vanilla
2 1/2 cups flour

Shape into balls and press thumb in center to create a hole for filling. Bake at 350 degrees for 15 minutes.

Cream filling:
8 ounces of cream cheese (softened at room temperature)
2 teaspoons vanilla
2 cups of powdered sugar
4 tablespoons flour

Cream together the above ingredients and fill the cookies.

Chocolate topping:
1 cup chocolate chips
4 tablespoons water
4 tablespoons margarine
1 cup of powdered sugar

Combine chocolate, water and margarine and place on low heat until chocolate is melted. Beat in powdered sugar. Cool and put a bit on the top of each cookie.

Decadent Chocolate Cookies

7 oz. semisweet chocolate
4 oz. bitter chocolate
6 tablespoons butter
1/3 cup flour
1/4 teaspoon baking powder
1/4 teaspoon salt
3 eggs
3/4 cup sugar
2 teaspoons vanilla
1 1/2 cups chocolate chips
1 cup pecans
1 cup walnuts

Melt semisweet chocolate with butter over low heat until smooth. Cool. Sift flour, baking powder, and salt together. Beat eggs, sugar and vanilla until fluffy. Add chocolate and then the flour mixture. Beat until blended. Stir in chips and nuts. Drop by tablespoon amounts onto lightly greased cookie sheets. Bake 10-12 minutes at 350 degrees.

This recipe comes to me from David Offenbach from New York.

REESES' PEANUT BUTTER BARS

1 cup butter, melted
2 1/2 cups powdered sugar
1 1/4 cups peanut butter
2 1/4 cups graham cracker crumbs

Mix together and put in a 9 x 13 pan. Melt 12 ounces of milk or dark chocolate chips and spread over bars. (About 1 teaspoon of Crisco shortening will keep the chips soft and glossy when added as you melt the chips.)

PUMPKIN BARS

2 cups sugar
2 cups pumpkin
4 eggs
1 cup oil
2 cups flour
2 teaspoons cinnamon
1/2 teaspoon salt
2 teaspoons soda

Mix all together and put in a greased 9 x 13 pan.

Frost when cool with:
8 ounce package cream cheese
1 stick butter
powdered sugar to sweeten

Almond Roca Cookies

1/2 pound butter
1/2 cup brown sugar
1/2 cup sugar (cream together)

Add:
1 egg yolk
1 tablespoon vanilla
2 cups cake flour

Put on buttered jelly roll pan-1/4" thick.
Bake 350 degrees for 15 minutes.

1 - 8 ounce bar sweet Chocolate-melted.
Spread this over warm cookies and top
with finely chopped toasted almonds. Cut
into squares while still warm. Cool until
chocolate sets before serving.

Rice Cookies

1 tablespoon honey
3 tablespoons sugar
1/4 pound butter (Boil together)

Add:
1 teaspoon vanilla
4 scant cups rice crispies

Put in a greased 9 x 13 pan-cut into squares
and put into refrigerator to set.

Whiskey Balls

3 1/2 cups crushed vanilla wafers
1 cup ground nuts
1 cup powdered sugar
3 tablespoons Karo syrup
1/2 cup bourbon

Roll in balls the size of a large cherry and
then in powdered sugar.

PIES & DESSERTS

LIN LEE'S FRENCH SILK PIE

3/4 cup sugar
1 stick butter
1 square unsweetened chocolate
1 teaspoon vanilla
2 eggs

Melt and cool chocolate. Cream butter and sugar, add chocolate and vanilla scraping sides of mixing bowl. Add eggs one at a time, beating 5 minutes after each egg, scrape bowl often. Pour into a 9 inch baked pie crust. Refrigerate. Cover with whipped cream, you can also grate chocolate bar over the top if desired.

HONEY BAKED APPLES

Core apples, use a tart green or red
Stuff lightly with brown sugar;
dot with butter;
fill cavity with honey and
sprinkle with cinnamon and stud with
    cloves

add 1/2 c. water to pan before baking

Bake in a 300 degree oven for 30 minutes.

PEARS POACHED IN RED WINE

3 cups dry red wine
1 cup sugar
1 stick cinnamon, broken into
    4 pieces
2 tablespoons vanilla
4 whole cloves
4 ripe pears, peeled

METHOD: Simmer pears in syrup about 12 minutes.

Chill at least 4 hours.

Cut pears in 1/2 lengthwise, remove cores, make lengthwise slits on the pears to make them fan out.

Put on serving plates; press down on pears to fan slices.

Serve with syrup.

CHOCOLATE NUT PIE

9" pie crust in pan unbaked

Place in bowl and beat all together:
1/4 cup butter
1 cup sugar
1/4 cup flour
1/3 cup cocoa
1/2 teaspoon salt
3 eggs (beat in one at a time)

Then add:
3/4 cup dark corn syrup
3/4 cup canned milk
1/2 cup chopped walnuts or pecans
3/4 teaspoon vanilla

Pour into 9" pie shell and bake at 450 for 10 minutes and 325 for 50 minutes.

This recipe comes from Tom's mother, Oasa Murphy.

CHOCOLATE MINT PIE

1 cup butter
2 cups powdered sugar
4 ounces semi-sweet chocolate
4 eggs
1 teaspoon peppermint extract
2 teaspoons vanilla

Beat together in order listed very thoroughly.

Crush 2 cups vanilla wafers for crust, mix with 1/2 cup butter and press into a 9 inch pie dish.

This is not cooked at all, but should be put in refrigerator to cool. A quick easy dessert, but delicious.

MIRACLE COBBLER

Start oven at 375 degrees - place 2 tablespoons butter in a quart baking dish and set in oven to soften. Allow it to cover bottom of dish and grease sides. Prepare a thin batter 1 cup flour, 1 cup sugar, 1 teaspoon baking powder, 1 cup milk, pinch of salt. Pour into buttered dish. Over batter spread 4 cups peaches (fresh or canned).

Bake at 375 degrees for 45 minutes. (Cherries, apricots, berries or black cherries may be used.) Serve warm with sauce made from fruit juice and a little corn starch, and butter.

LEMON BARS

1 cup butter
2 cups flour
1/2 cup powdered sugar
dash salt

Filling:
4 eggs
1 1/2 cups sugar
1/4 cup flour
6 tablespoons lemon juice
1 teaspoon lemon rind (grated finely)

METHOD: Mix butter, flour, and powdered sugar and salt together as for pie crust. Press into pan, bake in 9 x 13 pan for 15 minutes at 350 degrees.

Mix together filling and pour over crust. Bake for 25 minutes. Cool until set and then cut and place in cookie tin, or keep in pan.

This recipe comes from my friend Ellen Waldum of Livingston, Montana.

APPLE PIE

4 medium uncooked apples, peeled
    and quartered
1 unbaked crust
3/4 cup whipping cream
1/3 cup sugar
2/3 cup brown sugar
1 egg
1/8 teaspoon salt
3 tablespoons flour
3 teaspoons cinnamon
1 teaspoon nutmeg
1 teaspoon vanilla

Bake 450 degrees. Put apples in unbaked shell. Mix everything and pour over apples, cover with 2nd crust and bake 10 minutes at 450 degrees; reduce heat to 350 degrees for 30-45 minutes or until browned.

Old Fashioned Sour Cream Raisin Pie

1 cup raisins
1 cup thin sour cream
2 egg yolks, beaten
3 tablespoons flour
1 cup sugar
1/2 cup milk or juice from raisins
1 teaspoon vinegar
1/4 teaspoon salt

Cook raisins in enough water to cover. Combine sugar, flour, salt, vinegar, cream and milk or raisin juice. Cook over direct heat, stir constantly to keep from scorching. When thickened, spoon some of the mixture into the egg yolks and mix, now pour egg mixture into pudding slowly and stir while pouring. Allow to boil again and then add raisins. Pour into a baked pie shell. (Use egg whites for meringue)

No Roll Pie Crust

1 1/2 cups flour
1/2 cup vegetable oil
1 teaspoon sugar
3 tablespoon milk
1/4 teaspoon salt

Put flour in pie tin. Then mix all other ingredients with a fork until blended together. Pour into flour and mix well. Divide into 3 parts and press with finger to cover pie tin. These freeze very well.

Oil Pie Crust

1 1/2 cups flour
1/2 cup oil
2 tablespoons milk
1 teaspoon salt
1 tablespoon sugar

Put ingredients in 9" pie pan. Mix and pat into shape.

Bake 375 degrees for 10 min.

Pie Crust Mix

Sift together:
4 cups flour
1 teaspoon baking powder
1 teaspoon salt
1 tablespoon sugar

Blend in:
1 1/3 cups crisco
1/2 cup water
1 tablespoon vinegar
1 egg (beat together and add at once)

Toss quickly with a fork, will keep 2 weeks or longer in a refrigerator, and then can be rolled out and made into pie crusts.

This is not to be used as a savory or pasty dough. Use it only for sweet pies.

PEANUT BUTTER PIE

1 cup peanut butter
1 3/4 cups sugar
3 eggs
1 teaspoon vanilla
1/2 stick butter, melted
1 cup cream cheese

1 pint (2 cups) whipping cream
1 cup sugar

Fold top ingredients together - in different bowl whip cream and sugar until they form firm peaks, fold together. Pour into a high graham cracker pie crust. Refrigerate overnight. Before serving, drizzle with 1/2 cup chocolate chips melted with 1 teaspoon crisco, until blended.

TORTE LEMON DESSERT

Crust:
1 cup flour
2 tablespoons sugar
1/2 cup margarine

Blend and add:
1/2 cup finely chopped nuts

Cream Cheese Layer:
8 oz. cream cheese
cup powdered sugar
1 cup cool whip (blend together)

Pudding:
2 3 oz. pkg. instant lemon pudding
  mix
3 cups milk
rind of 1 lemon
juice of 2 lemons
add 1 cup cool whip, sprinkle with
  nuts or coconut

POTS d' CREME

1 cup chocolate chips, melted
beat into 6 egg yolks

Add:
2 teaspoons vanilla
2 ounces Creme de Cocoa
Fold in 6 egg whites, beaten stiff
chocolate for decoration

Put into pots d'creme cups or small goblets.
Chill 4 hours. Top with whipped cream.
Garnish with chocolate curls

GLAZED RASPBERRY PIE

3 boxes fresh raspberries
1 1/4 cups sugar
3 tablespoons cornstarch
1 tablespoon butter

Fill 9" baked pastry with 2 cups berries.
Mash the 1 cup berries add a little water,
the cornstarch and butter. Cook and strain
to remove the seeds. Add lemon juice to
make 1 cup then pour over fresh berries in
the baked crust.

QUICK SORBET

2 bags (16 oz.) frozen fruit
1 cup whipping cream
1/3 to 1/2 cup sugar
juice 1 lemon
1/2 cup cognac

Put all ingredients into blender

Freeze for at least 1/2 hour.

Pecan Pie

1/3 cup butter
3/4 cup brown sugar
dash of salt (cream together)

Add:
1 cup lite Karo
3 well beaten eggs
1 teaspoon vanilla
1 cup whole pecans

Pour into unbaked pie shell. Bake at 350 degrees for 15 minutes and 325 degrees for 30 minutes. Test as for custard.

Orange Lemon Pie

1 baked pie shell

Filling:
4 egg yolks, beat add
2 tablespoons sugar, beat add
5 tablespoons cornstarch blended with
1 cup sugar

Add:
4 tablespoons frozen orange juice concentrate
dash salt
1 cup boiling water
1 tablespoon butter, cook until thick

Meringue:
4 whites, beat until frothy add
1/4 teaspoon cream of tartar until soft peaks, add
1/2 cup sugar, 3 tablespoons at time until glossy, then add
1 tablespoon lemon juice.

Bake at 400 degrees for 10 minutes until meringue is brown and set.

GLAZED PEACH PIE

Prepare and bake 1 pie crust. I use the butter crunch crust. Slice enough fresh peaches to yield 2 1/2 cups. Sprinkle with 1 tablespoon lemon juice. Add 1/4 cup sugar and mix. Set aside for 1 hour. Drain peaches. Add enough water to juice to make 1 cup. Mix together in a pan 1/2 cup sugar and 3 tablespoons cornstarch. Cook rapidly, with the juice, until thick and clear.

Remove from heat, add 1/8 teaspoon salt and 1/8 teaspoon almond flavoring, also 2 tablespoons butter. Add the peaches. Turn into baked crust and cool. Serve with ice cream or whipped cream. Very good.

HAWAIIAN PIE

1 baked pie shell
1 package instant vanilla pudding
   (reg. size)
8 ounces crushed pineapple with
   juice
12 ounces sour cream
2 large tablespoons sugar
dash salt

Beat all together in mixer for 1 minute. Put in cool pie shell. Cover with whipped cream and top with chopped macadamia nuts or walnuts.

STRAWBERRY PIE

2 baked pie shells or graham cracker
   crusts

Filling:
2 egg whites - beat until fluffy
1 10 ounce package thawed frozen
   strawberries
1 cup sugar
1 tablespoon lemon juice

Beat on high for 15 minutes, after about 5 minutes divide into 2 bowls - beat each for balance of time - whip until thick. 1 cup whipping cream, add to the rest of the filling pile into shells. Put in freezer several hours before serving.

BUTTER CRUNCH PIE CRUST

1/2 cup butter
1/4 cup brown sugar, packed
1 cup sifted enriched flour
1/2 cup chopped pecans, walnuts or
    coconut

Heat oven to 400 degrees. Mix butter, brown sugar, flour, and nuts with hands. Spread in oblong pan, 9 x 13 1/2 x 2". Bake 15 min. Take from oven and stir. Press the hot Butter Crunch against bottom and sides of a 9" pie pan. Fill with favorite cream filling. (Chocolate is excellent). Top with meringue. Bake 5 to 10 minutes at 375 degrees. Serves 8.

EASY APPLE PIE

Fill a 8 x 8 pan with 3-4 cans of
    apple pie filling.

Mix together in a separate bowl:
1 cup sugar
1 cup flour
1 egg
1/4 cup butter
1/2 cup nuts
Sprinkle over the apples.

Bake 350 degrees for 50-55 minutes. Serve warm with fresh whipping cream or half and half.

FRENCH SILK CHOCOLATE TARTS

Cream together:
1/2 cup butter
3/4 cup sugar
1 ounce melted dark chocolate
1 teaspoon vanilla
2 eggs

Add eggs one at a time and beat for 5 minutes. Chill.

TART SHELLS

4 cups flour
1 teaspoon salt
1 teaspoon baking powder
1 tablespoon sugar
1 3/4 cups shortening
1/2 cup water
1 egg
1 tablespoon vinegar

This dough is easy to work with and is good for any tart. Baked tart shells will keep for up to 2 weeks packed in a tin away from light and heat.

Make as for pie dough. Use a 2 1/4 or 2 1/2 inch cookie cutter to make circles. Press in a tart pan or muffin pan, prick with a fork and bake at 425 degrees for 8 to 10 minutes.

This recipe was given to me by Amy Stephens of Livingston, Montana, a retired school teacher who is a native Montanan and wonderful cook.

Vanilla Pudding Dessert

Crust:
2 cups flour
2 cups coconut
1 cup butter
1/2 cup brown sugar

Brown in 9 x 13 pan at 350 for 15 minutes, then stir and bake for another 10 minutes. Cool. Prepare 3 packages instant vanilla pudding with 3 1/2 cups milk. Take out 1/2 of the cooled crumbs and place in another bowl. Spread the pudding on the crumbs, sprinkle with the rest of crumbs, cover with a big container of whipped topping or whipped cream and chill a half a day.

This comes from my favorite midwestern cook, Noreen Smith of Prior Lake, Minnesota.

Bonnie's Napoleons

1 sheet of Pepperidge Farm frozen Puff Pastry. Thaw pastry 20 minutes. Break the sheet into 3 pieces. Then cut these strips into 2" wide pieces. Bake 12-15 minutes at 350. Cool.

Make a cream custard following the directions on a package of Bird's custard powder, or if Bird's can't be found mix until very smooth a large package of instant vanilla pudding with a large carton of whipping cream, a little extra vanilla added. Cut 2 inch pastries in two and layer pudding and pastry in a stack with four pieces of pastry. Frost tops with a light frosting made from cream and powdered sugar, and drizzle with melted semi-sweet chocolate.

Robin Johnson's
Butterscotch Pie

1 1/4 cups brown sugar
2 cups milk
1/3 cup flour
1/8 teaspoon salt
3 eggs separated
2 tablespoons butter
1/2 teaspoon vanilla

Mix sugar and flour. Stir in milk. Heat slowly until boiling. Pour a small amount over the beaten egg yolks. Stir egg mixture back into sauce pan and boil for 3 minutes. Add remaining ingredients (excluding egg whites) and pour into an unbaked pie shell. Add six tablespoons powdered sugar into egg whites and beat until meringue forms. Spread over pie. Bake at 350 degrees until meringue browns. Chill at least 4 hours and serve cold.

Norwegian Apple Pudding

1/2 cup butter
1 cup sugar
1 cup sifted flour
2 teaspoons baking powder
1/4 teaspoon salt
1/2 teaspoon cinnamon
1/4 teaspoon cloves
1 cup milk
2 cups cooked fresh apples or one
    can of pie apples

METHOD: Melt the butter in the oven at 375 degrees in a 2 quart casserole, swish around to coat the bowl. Combine the next ingredients except for the apples and pour over melted butter. Drain apples and pile in center of the batter. Bake at 375 degrees until batter covers fruit and brown crust forms 30-40 minutes.

This comes to me from my cousin Noreen Smith in Minneapolis.

SALADS & DRESSINGS

ANTIPASTO PASTA SALAD

1 pound penne pasta
3 large roasted red peppers
2 jars marinated artichoke hearts,
    drained and coarsely chopped
1 cup provolone in fine slices
1 cup mushrooms, sliced
1/2 cup chopped red onion
1/3 cup chopped fresh basil
2/3 cup Caesar salad dressing
1 small can black olives, sliced
salt and fresh pepper

METHOD: Cook penne 10-12 minutes, drain and rinse in cold water. Add all the rest of ingredients - serve as fresh as possible.
Makes 8 servings.

CRUNCHY VEGETABLE SALAD

1 head cauliflower
1 head broccoli
3 to 4 stalks celery, diagonally sliced
1 package frozen peas, thawed with
    cold water and drained
1 pound bacon cooked, crumbled
    and drained on paper towels

Dressing:
2 cups Best Foods Mayonnaise (Lite)
1/4 cup sugar
1/4 cup Parmesan Cheese
2 teaspoons vinegar
1/4 cup minced onion
1/4 teaspoon salt

Preparations:
Make dressing and refrigerate. Wash and break up heads of cauliflower and broccoli into bite sized pieces.

Mix with sliced celery, thawed peas and drained bacon pieces. Toss in dressing; refrigerate until ready to serve for at least 1 hour.

This recipe comes from Dee Griffith of Spokane, WA.

CHINESE CHICKEN SALAD

Cook 3 chicken breasts in water with sliced fresh ginger 20 minutes or until tender. Drain and cool.

1 head shredded lettuce
1/2 package rice sticks (fried in oil, I use the wok for this)
bunch green onions (sliced thin)
1 small package sliced almonds toasted
1/4 cup toasted sesame seeds

Dressing:
4 tablespoons sugar
2 teaspoons salt (you can use 1)
1/4 teaspoons black pepper
4 tablespoons vinegar

Cook all of the above until sugar is melted. I usually make 4 times this amount and keep in fridge. When syrup is cool add 1/2 salad oil or sesame oil.

Pour the dressing over the salad just before serving; it does not keep well once the dressing is on it.

This recipe came to me from Cheryl Silk.

REFRESHING SUMMER PASTA SALAD

Small box thin spaghetti
1-16 ounce bottle of zesty Italian Dressing
1/2 pint of cherry tomatoes
small pieces fresh broccoli
small can of sliced black olives
thin sliced pepperoni
1/2 jar salad seasoning (Mrs. Dashes)

Cook spaghetti al dente. Add the rest of the ingredients and toss.

This recipe is from my cousin Noreen Smith from Minnesota.

Spicy Cauliflower

3 tablespoons olive oil
1 large chopped onion
1 head cauliflower florets
1 large clove garlic minced
1/2 cup chopped fresh basil
pinch of cloves
red pepper flakes
1 tablespoon each vinegar/water
6-8 ripe plum tomatoes
ground pepper

Put all the ingredients together and let it marinate for a bit.

Serves 6

Pasta Salad or Vegetable Salad

1 pound mastocciola
1 cup vinegar
1 cup oil
1 cup sugar
1/2 teaspoon salt
1 teaspoon seasoned salt
3/4 teaspoon pepper
1 teaspoon garlic powder
1 tablespoon onion flakes
1 tablespoon parsley flakes
2 large cucumbers
1 large green pepper, red pepper, yellow pepper mixed
2-3 tomatoes

optional:
broccoli, cauliflower, or mushrooms

Mix all together and let it sit.

This recipe is from my cousin Noreen Smith of Minnesota.

White Bean Salad

1 cup white cooked beans
1 cup chopped green onion
1 teaspoon minced garlic
2 tablespoons chopped parsley
2 tablespoons red wine vinegar
1/2 cup olive oil

Serve warm.

Green Beans Caesar

2 cans drained green beans (or
   equivalent of fresh cooked beans)
2 tablespoons salad oil
1 tablespoon vinegar
1 tablespoon minced onion
1 clove garlic, mashed

Toss beans with ingredients. Put into ungreased casserole.

Stir together: 2 tablespoons dry bread crumbs, 2 tablespoons grated Parmesan cheese, 1 tablespoons melted butter. Sprinkle crumbs over beans.

Bake uncovered at 350 degrees for 15-20 min.

This comes from my friend Irma Becker from the Black Hills.

HAP'S GREEN MEANY JELLO

1 large package green jello
1 large can crushed pineapple, well
  drained
3 tablespoons creamy horseradish

Cut water by 1/2 cup, but follow the package directions and add the other ingredients. The horseradish in this makes it a good accompaniment for lamb or pork roast.

My friend Hap Reubens always brings this for our traditional Christmas goose.

WHITVER'S LIME JELLO

1-3 ounce package lime jello
1 cup boiling water
7 ounce bottle 7-UP (can't be found
  these days, but a half a can of 7-up
  will do)
1 cup crushed pineapple
1 banana

Topping:
1/4 cup pineapple juice
1/4 cup sugar
1 tablespoon flour
1 beaten egg
1/2 cup whipping cream
1/4 cup shredded cheese

To make topping, combine sugar and flour in a saucepan, stir in pineapple juice and egg, cook until thickened. Whip cream - fold into egg mixture, spread over jello, top with cheese.

Slaw Dressing (Gram)

1 cup water
2 cups sugar
1 cup vinegar
1 teaspoon onion juice or grated
   onion
1 teaspoon salt
2 teaspoons celery seed
1 tablespoon mustard seed

Boil for 5 minutes. Remove from heat & add vinegar, onion juice or grated onion, salt, celery seed, mustard seed. Pour over a head of chopped cabbage which is tightly packed in a quart jar. Store in refrigerator.

Mandarin Lettuce Salad

2 tablespoons sugar
2 tablespoons vinegar
1/3 cup oil
dash of tabasco
white pepper
parsley
scallions
mandarin oranges
celery
can dried almonds
head Romaine lettuce

Make a dressing of the sugar, vinegar, and oil and tabasco. Put the rest of the ingredients into a salad. Toss with the dressing just before serving.

Ranch Dressing

2 teaspoons garlic salt
2 teaspoons onion salt
1 teaspoon pepper
2 teaspoons crushed parsley
1 quart mayonnaise
3 cups buttermilk

Put all in a large bowl and whisk together. Store in a jar in fridge. Will keep a long time.

Poppy Seed Dressing

1/4 cup sugar
1 tablespoon onion, grated
1 cup salad oil
1/3 cup cider vinegar
1 tablespoon poppy seed
1 teaspoon salt
1 teaspoon dry mustard

Use a whisk or a hand mixer to blend the salad oil into the mixture as you pour. If you don't blend as you pour, the dressing will separate.

Don Walters kindly shared this recipe from his collection.

Fruit Salad Dressing

1 egg, beaten
1/2 cup sugar
1 tablespoon cornstarch
1/2 cup pineapple juice, reserved
     from canned pineapple chunks
1/2 cup lemon juice, one whole
     lemon plus pineapple juice to make
     one cup liquid

Beat egg; add dry ingredients; add liquids; cook until thickened, stirring constantly. Cool. Use over a fruit salad mixed with canned pineapple chunks (save liquids for dressing); bananas, red apple & oranges.

This recipe come to me from Barbara Maxwell from CA.

CABBAGE SLAW

2 cups sugar
1 cup vinegar
1/2 cup water
1 teaspoon salt

Cabbage
2 red peppers
2 green peppers
chopped celery

1 1/2 teaspoons each celery seed
  and mustard seed.

Combine first four ingredients and boil for 5 minutes. Shred cabbage - soak in salted water 1 hour. Add to slaw: peppers, celery. Pour hot dressing over the cabbage. Add seeds at the end.

SESAME DRESSING

5 tablespoons sesame seeds
1/3 cup salad oil
1/2 teaspoon each of lemon peel,
  dry mustard
1/4 cup lemon juice
1 tablespoon sugar
1 tablespoon soy sauce
salt to taste

In a small frying pan - cook sesame seeds in salad oil over low heat until seed is golden, 5-8 min. Stir often. Let cool. Stir in remaining ingredients. Serve with chicken salad.

Fruit Salad Dressing

1 cup sugar
2 tablespoons cornstarch

Add:
Juice and rind of 1 orange
and enough water to make 1 cup

Cook until thick and clear, cool and add 1 cup whipped cream to this mixture.

Thousand Island Dressing

Take 1 cup Paul's cocktail sauce
add 1 cup mayonnaise

Sesame Seed Salad

Saute:
1/2 cup sesame seeds in 3
   tablespoons butter until nicely
   browned when cool

add:
1/2 cup grated Parmesan

Dressing:
1 cup sour cream
1/2 cup Best Foods Mayonnaise
1 tablespoon wine vinegar
1 tablespoon sugar
1 teaspoon each salt, garlic powder

Mix ingredients together then add dressing. Use one large head of Romaine or mixed lettuces - wash, drain, sprinkle with sesame seeds, add: celery, green pepper, green onions, avocado.

Chicken Fruit Salad

4 delicious apples, diced
2 cans pineapple chunks, drained
1 cup coconut
1 cup sliced almonds
5 cups diced chicken
2 cups diced celery

Dressing:
1/2 cup Best Foods mayonnaise
1 tablespoon chicken broth
1/2 teaspoon curry powder

Blend dressing first and toss with the rest of salad ingredients. Serves 8-10

Whipped Cream Dressing

1 cup cream, whipped with
4 tablespoons brown sugar

add:
2-3 tablespoons mayonnaise
3-4 tablespoons concentrated orange
  juice

CHINESE COLE SLAW

1/2 head green cabbage, slice very
   thin for slaw
1/2 head red cabbage, slice very
   thin for slaw
1 bunch green onions, slice thin and
   use tops
1 package chinese noodle flavor
   soup
1/2 cup slivered almonds and
2 tablespoons sesame seeds, both
   toasted in low oven

Make a dressing of the chicken flavoring from
the soup package with the following:
1/2 cup oil
3 tablespoons cider vinegar
2 tablespoons sugar
1/2 teaspoon each of salt and pepper

Shake this well in a jar and pour over cabbage. Add nuts and sesame seeds just before serving. Also add at this time the dry noodles from the soup mix. Break them up in a plastic bag first. This does not keep well, since the noodles get soggy.

This recipe was shared with me by Beverly Mulkey, Oregon

DON WALTER'S BROCCOLI SALAD

4 large heads broccoli, chopped fine
2 bunches green onion, chopped fine
1/2 pound bacon cooked until crispy
   and crumbled
1 pkg. yellow raisins
1 cup salted sunflower seeds

Put broccoli and green onion, bacon, and raisins in a large bowl.

Sauce:
2 cups mayonnaise
a little salt
4 tablespoons cider vinegar
3 tablespoons sugar

Pour over salad and mix well, then top with sunflower seeds.

LAYERED SALAD

1/2 head iceberg lettuce
1 10 ounce bag fresh spinach
4 eggs, hard cooked and chopped
1 bunch green onions chopped fine
1 pound bacon crispy fried and
  crumbled
1 10 1/2 ounce package frozen tiny
  peas (separated but not cooked)
1 or 2 tablespoons sugar
salt and pepper to taste
2 cups grated Swiss or cheddar
  cheese

Optional ingredients: water
  chestnuts, celery, tomato slices,
  radishes

Dressing:
1 1/2 cups sour cream
1 1/2 cups mayonnaise

Arrange vegetables in layers in 9 x 13 glass baking dish. Spread bacon evenly. Frost the top with dressing, spreading to edges of the dish to seal the casserole. Garnish with cheese. Cover with plastic wrap and refrigerate overnight to several days.

This recipe comes to me from my friend Barbara Maxwell of Bakersfield, California.

GRANDMA GRIFFITH'S COLESLAW

Take a large head of cabbage (this will feed 10-12 people) and shred it finely. (Soak in ice water until you are ready to serve, at least an afternoon. This makes the slaw crispy and sweetens the cabbage.) Shred also a large onion and 2 unpeeled cucumbers and set this aside in the fridge. Just before serving put onion and cukes with cabbage and pour the sauce over the cabbage. Serve while the cabbage is still crispy.

Sauce:
1 1/2 cups Hellman's mayonnaise
   (Best Foods in Rockies and the
   West)
4 tablespoons sugar
1 tablespoon celery seed
1/2 cup sour cream
light cream to make a thin sauce
   (this sauce should be the
   consistency of thick unwhipped
   whipping cream)
salt and pepper to taste

GRANDMA GRIFFITH'S POTATO SALAD

Cook 8-10 large baking potatoes with their skins still on in a large pan with ample water to cover them, add a tablespoon of salt. Cook them at least 1 hour or until well done. Cool peel and chop in a large bowl.

Dressing:
1 large sweet onion chopped
   coarsely (If you can't get your
   hands on sweet onions, a large
   white onion chopped and soaked
   in ice water for a few hours will
   work)
2 tablespoons yellow French's
   mustard
1 tablespoon Mutard d' Meaux or any
   other strong French country style
   mustard
2 cups mayonnaise
1 tablespoon celery seed
1 teaspoon onion salt
salt and pepper to taste

Mix this all up and pour over bowl of chopped potatoes, let this all rest for about an hour before you serve it. Serve at room temperature, but store in fridge in tightly covered bowl. Because this doesn't have egg in it, it will keep about a week in the fridge.

HOT CHICKEN SALAD EN CASSEROLE

2 cups diced chicken
2 cups chopped celery
1/2 cup almond flakes (toasted for 5
   minutes at 400 degrees)
1/3 cup chopped green pepper
2 tablespoons minced green onion
1/2 teaspoon salt
2 tablespoons lemon juice
2 cups crushed potato chips
1 cup mayonnaise
1/3 cup grated cheese

Blend chicken, celery, almonds, green pepper, onion, salt, lemon juice and mayo. Put alternate layers of chicken mixture and crushed potato chips in buttered casserole. Top with layer of chips and grated cheese mixed together. Bake at 350 degrees for about 20-30 minutes.

This recipe is from my Grandmother Griffith's old cookbook from a Women's Club in Iowa. I doubled this recipe for the 10 of us and we could have used even more. I expect you would triple it for a group of ten to have ample.

SALMON SALAD

Poach a Salmon, cool it in fridge. Break into chunks and add green onions, capers, and chives. Serve with Mustard Dill Sauce.

IOWA CUCUMBER SALAD

Run a fork down 4 large cucumbers. Slice very thinly.

Cover with the following dressing:
1 cup sour cream
2 tablespoons sugar
1/2 cup mayonnaise
1 bunch green onions
3 tablespoon vinegar (this is an
    estimate)
salt and pepper to taste

REFRIGERATOR COLESLAW

1 medium head cabbage
1 medium carrot
1 green pepper
1 onion
1 teaspoon salt
Run all of this through the food processor pulsing with the steel blade.

Dressing:
1 cup vinegar
1/4 cup water
2 cups sugar
1 teaspoon each of celery and
    mustard seed

Combine these ingredients and boil for one minute. Cool to lukewarm and pour over vegetables. Put in quart jars in freezer of fridge. This will make 2 quarts. I will double or triple this recipe and then keep it in freezer. Use this as a condiment with ham or other sliced meats on sandwiches or as a side dish salad.
This can also be frozen in quart jars.

DON WALTER'S
SWEET POTATO SALAD

4 1/2 cups sweet potatoes (2 cans)
4 hard boiled eggs chopped finely
2 bunches of chopped green onions
2 stalks of celery

Mash together and then add dressing:
3/4 cup Best Foods Mayonnaise
  (Hellman's out East)
1/2 cup Durkees Dressing
1 teaspoon sweet pickle juice
2 tablespoons sugar
2 tablespoons brown sugar
2 tablespoons cider vinegar
2 tablespoons light cream
1/4 teaspoons dry mustard
about 1/4 teaspoon each salt and
  pepper

Let this stand in the refrigerator overnight or at least for several hours so the dressing can flavor the potatoes.

VEGETABLES

BROCCOLI
(WITH SESAME AND LEMON)

Clean a large bunch of broccoli. Make into florets. Put a large pan of water to boil, when boiling add broccoli and boil for 8 minutes until crisp and bright green. Do not over cook. Toss with toasted sesame seeds and sesame oil (about 2 Tablespoons) and then sprinkle with fresh lemon.

To toast sesame seeds, put in a dry heavy pan on flame or burner and over medium heat keeping the pan moving to brown them. They sometimes pop like popcorn, but most will stay in the pan.

HASSELBACK POTATOES

Use one large baking potato for each serving + 1 or 2 extra for your big eaters. Scrub the potatoes as for baked potatoes. Using a large spoon, place the potato in the spoon and then cut the potato in thin slices without cutting all the way through. Put them on a buttered pan and brush them with melted butter, sprinkle them with garlic and onion salts, or seasoning salt, basil or any herbs you like on potatoes. Bake them in a 400 degree oven for 45 minutes then take them out and brush them with butter again, sprinkle them with dry bread crumbs, and pour extra butter over the crumbs (all this buttering takes about 2 sticks of butter for 10-12 servings).

GREEN BEAN BUNDLES

For each bundle:
6 beans (fresh crisp beans)
wrap with 1/2 piece partially cooked
bacon
sprinkle with garlic salt
4 tablespoons butter (sprinkle over
beans)
3 tablespoons brown sugar

Put the bundles in a glass pyrex dish, in a single layer.

Bake at 350 degrees for 15-20 minutes.

COLD DILLED PEAS

10 oz. tiny peas, cook minimally and
drain
1 cup sour cream
1 tablespoon dill weed
1 teaspoon chopped chives
salt and pepper
1 teaspoon curry powder
fresh lemon juice

Chill and serve as a salad.
Garnish with fresh dill.

SWEET AND SOUR GREEN BEANS

1/2 pound bacon, cooked crisp and
crumbled
1 1/2 cups brown sugar
1/2 cup vinegar
big onion diced
Simmer brown sugar, vinegar, and
onion together 25 min.
4 cans cut green beans, or 1 can
each: kidney, navy, lima, pork and
beans

Partially drain beans, and put them in a greased casserole.

Bake about 45 minutes at 350 degrees.

MASHED POTATOES WITH CARAMELIZED ONIONS AND CABBAGE

Sauté:
4 tablespoons unsalted butter
2 large onions, thinly sliced
3 cups thin sliced cabbage (1/2 small head)

Boil:
2 pounds Russet potatoes with a little salt and mash with
1/3 cup half and half
Mix 1 cup onion mixture into potatoes

Heat oven to 375 degrees, and put potato and onion mixture in a greased casserole.

2 tablespoons red wine vinegar
1 tablespoon water

Add vinegar and water to the rest of the onion in skillet.
Cook until moisture is gone.

Spoon over casserole, bake 30 minutes.

Makes 4 Servings.

MASHED POTATOES WITH CABBAGE AND CHEDDAR CHEESE

1/2 head of green cabbage (shredded finely)
2 1/2 pounds russet potatoes
1/2 stick unsalted butter
1/4 cup fresh chives or green onion tops
1 cup grated cheddar cheese (4 oz.)

METHOD: Cook cabbage 2 minutes in boiling water, transfer using slotted spoon, drain. Return water to boil add potatoes and cook until tender.

Mash the potatoes, mix in chives/cabbage.

Spoon into buttered serving dish, sprinkle with cheese. Bake at 350 degrees, heated until cheese bubbles, about 35 min.

POTATOES FOR A CROWD

5 pounds potatoes
1 pint Whipping Cream
salt

Boil potatoes in skins in salted water. Grate into a thickly buttered 9 x 13 pan. Pour carton of whipping cream over them, dot with butter.

Bake 350 degrees until nicely browned, about one hour.

MISSISSIPPI POTATOES

8 cups potatoes (cooked and diced)
1 cup mayonnaise
1 teaspoon salt
1/2 teaspoon pepper
1 pound grated cheddar cheese
4 to 6 slices fried bacon (crumbled)
1/2 cup olives green or black

Bake 325 degrees for 1 hour, can make ahead to freeze; thaw before cooking.

4 C's Potatoes

2 packages frozen hashbrown shreds
1/2 cup butter
1 tablespoon salt
1/4 teaspoon pepper
1/2 cup chopped green onions
1 can mushroom soup
1 cup milk
1 cup sour cream
1 1/2 cups grated cheddar cheese

Mix all together and bake in a greased 9 x 13 pan 1 1/2 hours at 350 degrees.

Make Ahead Mashed Potatoes

9 large baking potatoes peeled and cut into chunks cooked in salted water until soft.
1/2 cup butter
12 ounces cream cheese at room temperature
1/2 cup sour cream
Pinch of nutmeg
1/4 teaspoon white pepper
1/2 teaspoon salt

Mash the potatoes and add the rest of the ingredients (cut the cream cheese in chunks). Scrape into a heavily buttered casserole and refrigerate, covered with plastic wrap. To cook, bring to room temperature and reheat at 300 degrees, uncovered, for about 20 minutes.

Barbara Maxwell gave me this recipe.

ENTREES

Three Green Pasta with Scallops and Pesto Sauce

1 pound asparagus
(1 1/2 inch pieces), lightly sauté
1/2 pound fresh green beans
(cook 5 minutes and sauté in a
little olive oil until tender crisp.)
1 pound fettucini, boil in vegetable
water, drain and set aside
3 tablespoons butter
1 10 oz. package frozen peas (barely
cook and set aside)

2 pounds scallops, quartered. Sauté
1 minute.

Make a sauce of:
1 1/2 cups pesto
3/4 cups whipping cream
2 tablespoons fresh lemon juice
(quickly add the vegetables and
serve over pasta)

Makes 8 servings.

Spicy Pot Roast

Take a 3-4 pound pot roast, let it sit in the refrigerator on a rack covered with a tea towel for at least 4 days. On the 4th day brown the pot roast on all sides in olive oil; then add:

1 small can tomato sauce
1 cup dry red wine
2 pieces orange peel (orange part
only 1" x 2")
5 whole cloves
2 cinnamon sticks
2 cloves garlic minced
12 small white onions

Bake at 325 degrees for 3 hours, during the last hour add the small white onions. Remove the roast and let it sit while you make gravy over the drippings.

Makes 6-8 servings.

Pork Stew with Mushrooms & White Wine

2 1/2 pounds boneless pork
1 tablespoon oil
1 tablespoon butter
2 onions, chopped
2 tablespoons flour
1 cup dry white wine
2 cups chicken broth
2 cloves garlic, minced
3 shallots, chopped
2 tomatoes, peeled, seeded,
  and chopped
1 bay leaf, 2 thyme sprigs,
2 parsley sprigs
salt and pepper
3/4 pounds mushrooms, quartered

Cut the pork into 1 1/2" cubes. In a heavy casserole, heat the butter and oil and fry the pork cubes until thoroughly browned on all sides. Remove them, add the onions and brown them too. Stir in the flour and brown it also. Note: it is this thorough browning that gives flavor to the stew. Pour in wine and bring it to a boil. Stir in stock, spices, shallots, tomatoes, garlic, salt & pepper and pork. Cover the casserole, bring to a boil and cook in a 350 degree oven 1 to 1 1/2 hours until the pork is tender. Stir occasionally and add stock if necessary. Add mushrooms and continue to cook until mushrooms are tender and meat is almost falling apart. If sauce is too thin, boil to reduce. (I use a 1 lb. can of tomatoes, drained. Make the day before and reheat. Delicious.)

Bob Chaplick sent me this recipe knowing it would travel well in the field.

GREEK CHOPS

10 pork chops (loin)
salt & pepper

Brown in olive oil and garlic until seared.
Layer in baking dish. Slice 3 lemons thinly
and lay on top of the chops. Sprinkle with
fresh thyme and juice of 2 lemons. Bake 1
1/2 - 2 hours at 350 degrees.

NOODLE PUDDING

1 pound fine noodles (cooked and
   drained)
6 eggs
6 ounces cream cheese
2 1/4 cups milk
3/4 cup sugar
3/4 pound cottage cheese
10 tablespoons butter

After noodles have been cooked and
drained add the remaining ingredients. Top
with crushed graham cracker crumbs. Cook
in well greased pans for 45 to 60 minutes at
350 until golden brown.

BBQ Ribs

1/8 teaspoon garlic powder
1/2 cup ketchup
1/3 cup chili sauce
2 tablespoons brown sugar
1 teaspoon celery seed
2 tablespoons chopped onion
1 tablespoon mustard
1 tablespoon Worcestershire
1/4 teaspoon salt
1 tablespoon lemon juice
hot sauce (a few drops)

Simmer together. I usually quadruple this recipe using a whole bottle of chili sauce and then store it in quart jars in the fridge. It keeps a long time. To make the ribs, choose meaty pork ribs and simmer them for about 1 hour, a huge pan of them takes more time, with a little salt. Take the ribs out and put them on greased foil lined cookie sheets. Smear them with the sauce and let them sit and brood for a couple of hours at least. Then bake them or stick them under the broiler to sear and serve immediately.

SPINACH AND CHICKEN ENCHILADAS

1 medium sour cream
1 can cream of mushroom soup
longhorn cheddar cheese (shredded)
1 can mild chopped green chilies
cooked chopped chicken / turkey
1 package chopped spinach (cooked)
1 dozen flour tortillas (or crepes)
cumin, garlic to taste

Mix together soup, sour cream, cheese, chilies, chicken or turkey, spinach, and seasonings. Roll 2-3 abundant tablespoons in each tortilla and place seam side down in oiled dish. After these are baked, top with sour cream, cheese, black olives, or whatever you have.

Bake 350 degrees for 20-30 minutes until heated through.

This recipe comes to me from Sally King. Her husband is the Chief ranger at Glacier Bay Park in Alaska.

Taco Filling

3 pounds lean ground beef
6 cloves garlic, finely minced
1 large onion, chopped fine
5 jalapeño chilies, chopped up finely
8 ounces tomato sauce
1 can beef broth
1 tablespoon oregano
1 teaspoon thyme
1 large pinch dried coriander
salt & pepper

Heat meat until pink color is gone - strain it over bowl. Let sit, when meat is dripped out use 2-3 tablespoons of the fat, onion, garlic, and peppers, simmer adding beef broth if it looks dry, simmer for at least an hour with a light lid.

This recipe comes from my friend Hap Reubens, who lived extensively in Mexico.

Cornish Game Hens

2 tablespoons butter
2 tablespoons sugar
3 tablespoons orange juice
   concentrate
3 tablespoons currant jelly
1/8 teaspoon garlic powder
pinch salt

Cut hens in half and sprinkle with lemon juice / salt / pepper.

Bake at 400 degrees for 30 minutes. Combine all glaze ingredients. Cook until sugar and jelly are dissolved about 10 min. after boiling point. Spoon glaze over hens return to oven 350 degrees for 30 min.

SIS POLIN'S BRISKET

onions
one fresh brisket
1 package Lipton onion soup
1 cup ketchup (or chili ketchup)
carrots
celery
1 cup red wine (optional)

Slice onions and cover bottom of baking pan. Put on top of brisket (remove fat). Sprinkle on top Lipton onion soup, ketchup (or chili ketchup). Throw in cut up carrots and celery add red wine (optional). COVER! Bake at 325 degrees until meat is tender. Remove meat, place remaining of ingredients in blender and puree. Put in freezer, remove fat. Slice meat against grain, warm in pureed gravy.

CHICKEN CIDER STEW

2 cups apple cider
3 tablespoons catsup
2 slices bacon, cut up
1 1/2 teaspoon salt
1/4 teaspoon dried savory, crushed
1/4 teaspoon dried basil, crushed
1/8 teaspoon pepper
1 2-3 pound chicken cut up
4 carrots, thinly sliced
2 medium sweet potatoes, peeled
   and cubed
2 medium onions, finely chopped
1 stalk celery, cut into 1 inch pieces
1 apple, peeled, cored and chopped
3 tablespoons flour

METHOD: In a large kettle stir together the first 7 ingredients. Add chicken. Bring to boiling, reduce heat, cover and simmer for about 45 minutes. Stir in carrots, sweet potatoes, onions, celery and apple. Cover and simmer about 30 minutes or until meat and vegetables are tender. Blend the flour and 1/4 cup cold water; stir into hot stew. Cook until mixture is thickened and bubbly.

This recipe is from Don Walters.

Fettuccine Romana

2 tablespoons extra virgin oil
1 medium yellow onion, peeled and
chopped
3 cloves garlic, peeled and minced
2 carrots, peeled and finely chopped
2 stalks celery, finely chopped
3/4 pound hot Italian sausage
1 meaty short rib, about 1 pound
1/2 pound ground beef
1/2 pound ground pork
2 cups dry red wine
2 28 ounce cans Italian style whole
tomatoes
8 ounces porcine mushrooms
salt and freshly ground black pepper
2 pounds dried fettuccine
Parmigiana reggiano

Step 1: Heat oil in a large skillet over medium heat. Add onions, garlic, carrots, and celery, and cook until soft, about 15 minutes.

Step 2: Remove sausage from casing, break up, and add to vegetables. Cut meat off short rib, chop into bite-size pieces, and add, with short rib bone, beef, and pork, to vegetables and sausage. Brown meat for 20 min.

Step 3: Add wine, increase heat to high, and cook, uncovered, for 20 minutes. Stir in tomatoes, crushing them with the back of a spoon. Reduce heat to low, and simmer, partially covered, for 45 minutes. Add water if needed.

Step 4: Chop and add mushrooms. Cook uncovered, until thick, at least 45 minutes more. Season to taste with salt and pepper.

Step 5: Bring a large pot of salted water to a boil over medium high heat. Add fettuccine and cook until al dente, 8-10 min. Drain in a colander and transfer while hot to a large serving bowl and toss with sauce.

Serve topped with parmigiana reggiano and garnished with short-rib bone, if desired.

This recipe comes from a little restaurant in Assisi, Italy. I asked for it. I have fiddled with it for about 5 years.

LEMON CHICKEN

1 chicken in pieces - soak in 6
   tablespoons lemon juice / then
   flour
Brown in butter in a skillet
Season with salt, pepper and mix
   together with:
1 cup hot water
1/4 cup green onion
1 tablespoon white sugar
1 tablespoon brown sugar
remaining lemon juice
2 tablespoons chicken bouillon

Pour over the chicken and cook on the top of the stove until the chicken is done. About 1 hour.

BAKED CHICKEN

1 cut up frying chicken
dip in sour cream or mayonnaise
roll in crushed potato chips
season lightly with pepper

Put on a buttered jelly roll pan and bake at 350 degrees for 1 1/2 hours.

Oven Baked Rice

1/4 cup butter
1 cup long grain rice
Saute to a golden brown and add:
1 can chicken broth
1 3/4 cups water
1 teaspoon salt

Put in a covered Casserole. Bake 1 hour at 350 degrees. May be prepared the day before - refrigerate unbaked, 1 1/4 hours to bake then.

Sis Polin's Easy Potato Knishes

Defrost Pepperidge Farm Puff Pastry
Peel, cut up and boil about 5 pounds of potatoes until soft.
Slice 1 or 2 large onions and saute until brown in vegetable oil.
Mash potatoes with a little salt and lots of black pepper.

Roll out puff pastry. Spread with potato and onion mixture and roll in jelly roll fashion. Cut into 2" pieces. Set on oiled cookie sheet, cut side down and pinch other side together. Bake 350 until brown (around 1/2 hour). These can be prepared ahead, placed on a cookie sheet and frozen. Thaw slightly and bake at a later time.

SAUSAGE FILLED CREPES

Crepes:
3 eggs
1 cup milk
1/2 teaspoon salt
1 tablespoon oil
1 cup flour

Filling:
1 pound pork sausage
1/2 cup chopped onion
1/2 cup shredded cheddar cheese
3 ounces cream cheese
1/4 teaspoon marjoram

Crepes:
Beat until smooth. Cook on one side only and invert on toweling.

Filling:
Brown sausage and the other ingredients. Roll up crepes with sauce filling and put in an 11 x 13 pan, cover and chill. Bake at 375 degrees for 40 minutes.

Beat together:
1/2 cup sour cream
1/2 cup soft butter

Spread over crepes and bake an additional 5 minutes.

BONNIE'S WHITE SAUCE FETTUCCINE

1 tablespoon olive oil
1/2 stick butter
1 cup sour cream
1/2 cup freshly grated Parmesan cheese
1 teaspoon salt
pinch of black pepper

Melt butter, stir in sour cream until blended; simmer for 1 minute to thicken. Toss with about 1/2 pound of fettuccine, the fresh parmesan, and salt and pepper.

NORWEGIAN MEATBALLS
FOR A CROWD

4 pounds lean ground beef
2 eggs
1 teaspoon each of ground allspice,
   ground cloves, and ground
   cardamom
1 large onion chopped very fine
salt and pepper to taste

Make a zillion little meatballs and brown them on sided cookie sheets in the oven for about 15 minutes. Put them aside. Scrape all the drippings into a large pan and cover with milk to make a gravy. Add flour mixed with milk, salt and pepper to thicken the gravy, then add the meatballs just until warm. Serve with Hasselback potatoes.

HAM

Take a very large ham and cover it with a mixture of 1 cup of brown sugar, 2 teaspoons of dry mustard, and about 1 teaspoon of ground cloves. Use this as a paste on the ham. Put the ham in a covered large pan and then pour over it a bottle of any good beer. Cook for 6-7 hours in a slow oven. Watch - the beer will burn if the oven is too high or it runs out of liquid.

STAN WATT'S FRANCHISABLE PIZZA

3 Boboli or large pizza crusts
Chop:
9 garlic cloves
3 large red onions
3 red peppers
3 yellow peppers

2 pounds ground bison or elk meat
1 pound hot Italian sausage
1 large can black olives, chopped
1 jar artichoke hearts, chopped
3 tablespoons chopped fresh basil

Blend together and set aside:
2 pounds mozzarella cheese, grated
1 carton freshly grated parmesan
   cheese

Saute the garlic and onions lightly in a little olive oil and brush on the Boboli or pizza crust, bake for 5 minutes in a 450 degree oven, to set the crust.

Saute onions and peppers lightly, drain thoroughly.

Separately saute bison, and then Italian sausage, drain thoroughly.

Assemble pizzas by putting on first the meat, then the veggies, then the olives and artichokes, they will be loaded with ingredients. Then top the works with the cheeses, covering generously.

Bake in a hot oven, 400 degrees, 15-20 minutes until the cheeses are melted but not browned.

Serve hot or cold. Serves 10 people.

I am calling this Stan Watt's pizza, because he said I could make a fortune in New Jersey selling these pizzas. Have a go Stan.

EGGPLANT LASAGNE

Two 9 x 13 glass casseroles
1 box Lasagne, cook as directed, add
a little oil to the boiling water, and
set aside
3 eggplants: peel and slice in 1/2
inch slices.

Brush with oil and put on a baking sheet and bake in a hot oven for about 30 minutes or until tender.

Sauce:
12 oz. can tomato paste
cup of good red wine
6 cloves chopped garlic
salt and pepper to taste

Simmer sauce about 20 minutes
then add:
3 chopped green peppers
can or two of chopped black olives
Fry up some good Italian Sausage
(Hot!) and drain off fat

To assemble:
Spray a 9 x 13 pan and layer first lasagne, then eggplant, meat, then cheese Parmesan and mozzarella, and then pour sauce over and layer again.

Bake at 350 degrees for about 30 minutes, let set up before serving.

QUESADILLAS

8 10" flour tortillas
1 cup chopped ham
2 cups shredded cheddar cheese or
   feta
1/2 cup chopped cilantro
1 cup crushed pineapple

Serve with mango salsa:
2 ripe mangoes - peeled, seeded,
   sliced
2 tablespoons minced red onion
1 tablespoon fresh cilantro
1 serano chili, minced
1/4 cup fresh lime juice

Place one flour tortilla on lightly greased grilling pan, add the ham, cheese, cilantro, and pineapple liberally, cover with another tortilla and grill briefly, being careful to turn the tortilla over without spilling out the contents. The cheese melted helps this process.

Cornish Pasties

2 1/4 cups flour
1 teaspoon salt
3/4 cup lard, do not substitute for
   the lard
4-5 tablespoons ice water

Filling:
1/2 pound ground beef or finely
   chopped steak
1 1/2 cups diced raw potato
3 tablespoons chopped onion
1 1/2 tablespoons salt & pepper

Roll out as for pie dough. Cut in 4" circles. Fill with filling and fold over crimping edge tightly. Brush with beaten egg.

Bake at 450 degrees for 20 minutes, then 375 degrees for 20 minutes. Serve with brown gravy. I save left over brown gravy in the freezer to use with pasties.

DEEP SOUTH BAKED CHICKEN

1 fryer cut up
1 cup bisquick
1 1/2 teaspoons salt
1 teaspoon paprika
1/2 teaspoon poultry seasoning
1/2 cup chopped pecans
1/2 cup milk
1/2 cup melted butter

Rinse and pat dry chicken, combine ingredients, dip chicken in milk, then in pecan mixture. Arrange in a greased 9 x 13 baking dish, pour melted butter over. Bake 375 degrees for about 1 hour, uncovered.

BAKED CHICKEN BREASTS

6 breasts–12 pieces
Marinade:
marinate overnight in 2 cups sour
   cream - room temperature
1/4 cup lemon juice
1 tablespoon Worcestershire sauce
2 cloves garlic
2 teaspoons celery salt
2 teaspoons paprika
salt / pepper

TO COOK: Melt 1 stick of butter in 9 x 13 glass baking dish - roll marinated pieces in one cup dry bread crumbs, place in baking dish, pour rest of butter over the top.

Bake for 45 minutes at 350 degrees. Then cover and bake 20 minutes longer. Let stand 10 minutes before serving.

SOUPS

CHICKEN AND BARLEY SOUP

On the day before you need the soup, put a whole chicken in a pot with about 3 quarts of water. Add 6 garlic cloves, a large onion chopped up and 2 tablespoons salt and about 1/2 teaspoon of peppers. Simmer the chicken for about 3 hours. Set aside to cool.

The next day, skim off the fat, cut up the meat and discard bones and skin. Set meat aside. Heat up all the broth and add a little water if necessary, then add all chopped into chunks, 6 large carrots, 6 potatoes, 3 stalks of celery, 1/2 cup barley, 1 bay leaf and extra salt and pepper and 1 teaspoon dried sage. Cook for about 1 hour and then add the chicken and cook just until hot. Garnish with green onion.

KING SALMON CHOWDER

2 pounds Alaskan salmon
1 quart 1/2 and 1/2
package of chives
5 pounds of potatoes
2 bunches green onion chopped
2 tablespoons butter
2 tablespoons salt
pepper to taste

In a large soup stock kettle: Brown chopped onion in butter and then add chopped potatoes, some of the chives, salt, and pepper. Add water to cover the potatoes and cook the potatoes until tender, about 30 minutes.

Poach the salmon until tender (about 7 minutes or less) in a steamer pan or frying pan with just a little water. De-bone the salmon and set pieces aside. Just before serving add the salmon and cream and the fish juice. Season it with chopped green onion or chives just before serving.

Chicken Soup with Corn Tortillas

1 package corn tortillas
halved or cut in thin strips,
deep fry in a little oil

Soup: Sauté
1 large finely chopped onion
3 cloves chopped garlic
2 tablespoons chili powder
3 teaspoons ground cumin
1 teaspoon dried oregano
1 bay leaf
8 cups chicken broth
1 small can tomato sauce
1 teaspoon salt
pepper

Add:
2 large chicken breasts, cut into
    bite sized pieces
2 cups frozen corn

Cook until breast pieces are tender, about
10 minutes.

This will feed 5 people. I double this recipe
for a larger crowd.

Minestrone Soup

On the day before you need the soup, cook a large pan full of soup bones or a large chuck roast cut up with several cloves garlic and a large chopped onion and 2 tablespoons of Italian herbs and about 2 tablespoons salt and a little pepper. Cook it covered with water for about 6 hours on a simmer. Set it in a cold place to cool.

The next day skim off almost all the fat, bone the meat, and chop it up. Set it aside, Heat and strain the broth into a new kettle, and add 2 large cans chopped up tomatoes with their juice, 1 large can tomato sauce, and a small can tomato paste. Add 2 more tablespoons of Italian herbs, about 6 large potatoes cut into chunks, 2 cans garbanzo beans, a can of green beans cut in pieces, and some parsley. Cook for about an hour on simmer, then add the meat and pasta (shells are nice) and cook for another half an hour. Serve hot with parmesan cheese.

CREAMY MUSHROOM AND CHICKEN SOUP

1 ounce porcine mushrooms - dried
   (Soak the mushrooms until they
   can be easily sliced)
8 slices bacon, chopped, sauteed
   discard the fat

Saute:
1 onion chopped
2 cloves garlic
1 teaspoon dried thyme
1/2 pound fresh mushrooms,
   chopped
1/4 cup flour
6 cups chicken stock
1 cup dry white wine
1 tablespoon tomato paste
1 bay leaf
1 pound chicken meat

Just before serving add:
1 1/2 cups whipping cream

Serve with French bread

Use chopped fresh parsley and green onion
as garnish.

CHICK PEA SOUP WITH GARLIC AND HERBS

1 1/2 pounds dried chick peas
   (soak in cold water overnight)
6 tablespoons olive oil
1 chopped large onion
7 fresh sage leaves
or 1 1/2 teaspoons dried sage
3 garlic cloves minced

Simmer chick peas at least 3 hrs. with the
ingredients at left.

Serve with:
   croutons
   chopped red onion
   sweet and fruity olive oil

COCONUT CHICKEN SOUP

3 14 oz. cans unsweetened coconut
  milk (lite is fine)
2 cups chicken broth
1 cup canned straw mushrooms
  (drained)
1/4 cup chopped fresh lemongrass or
  dried lemon grass
1 1/2 tablespoons minced peeled
  fresh ginger
1 tablespoon brown sugar
1 1/2 teaspoons minced fresh
  jalapeño chili
1/4 cup chopped cilantro
2 tablespoons fresh lime juice
8 oz. boneless chicken breast, thinly
  sliced

Mix all together. (Add lime juice last, just before serving.) Heat until chicken breast is cooked, about 10 minutes.
Serves 4.

FOUR CHEESE SOUP

1/2 stick unsalted butter
1 medium leek (white, light green
  chopped)
8 cups chicken broth
2 medium russet potatoes, peeled
  and diced
1 quart half and half
1 1/2 cups each grated provolone,
  parmesan, mozzarella, cheddar
  (or any four you especially like or
  have on hand).

Melt butter in heavy saucepan over medium heat, saute leek add stock and potatoes. Bring to boil and then simmer 25 minutes, puree, add half and half. Gradually add cheese to soup until it is well blended and the soup is hot, but not boiling. Serve immediately.

6 servings

POTATO, LENTIL AND MUSHROOM SOUP

2 tablespoons olive oil
1 1/2 cups chopped green onion
2 pounds russet potatoes, cubed
4 cans beef broth
1 pound mushrooms, chopped
Kielbasa Sausage - cut in pieces
1 1/2 cups lentils, rinsed and drained
1 1/2 teaspoons dried thyme

METHOD: Cook potatoes and lentils 1 1/2 hours.

Puree some of soup to thicken (Can be made 2 days ahead, and refrigerated with good results.)

Makes 6-8 servings

SAUSAGE ONION SOUP UPTOWN CAFE

1 pound Italian sausage (hot or sweet or mix of both), cut into 1 inch pieces
2 tablespoons olive oil
1 large Spanish onion (about 3/4 pound), chopped coarsely
2 teaspoons minced garlic
1/4 cup firmly packed light brown sugar
1/2 cup dry white wine
2 tablespoons Dijon mustard
8 cups beef broth
2 tablespoons minced fresh flat-leafed parsley leaves plus additional for garnish

1. In a heavy kettle saute sausage in oil over moderately high heat, stirring, until browned, about 3 minutes. Pour off fat and add onion and garlic. Cook 3 to 5 minutes, or until onion is softened.
2. Add remaining ingredients and simmer with cover ajar 1 hour.
3. Add salt and pepper to taste. Serve soup garnished with parsley.

Makes about 10 cups.

SPAETZLE

1 cup + 2 tablespoons flour
1 teaspoon salt
1 egg
1/2 cup milk

Mix together lightly and press through slotted spoon into boiling beef or chicken soup.

This recipe comes to me from Sharon Farell of Livingston.

EGG NOODLES

3 eggs / slightly beaten

add:
2 teaspoons cooking oil
2 teaspoons water
1 teaspoon salt

add:
about 1 cup flour

Roll out in 2 batches, slice in thin slices and dry on a tea towel over the back of a chair.

These noodles can be used in any casserole asking for noodles, or as the noodles in chicken noodle soup. You'll never buy another can of Campbells.

MEATBALL SOUP

1 1/4 pound ground round
1/2 cup raw rice
3-4 cups diced celery
1 large onion diced
1 large can tomato juice
2 large cans tomatoes, crushed
4-5 cups water

Mix rice and raw meat, season. Form small balls, about 20. Bring water and juice to a boil. Add celery, onion and meatballs. Simmer slowly 45 minutes to an hour. Turn off heat and add tomatoes. Reheat.

Serves 6

This recipe comes from John & Beth Ross of Madison, WI.

COLD CARROT GINGER SOUP

2 large carrots in chunks
(Microwave for 15 minutes with
   butter and 1/4 cup water)

Puree in food processor with:
1 can cream of chicken soup
1 can water
1 cup chicken broth
1 cup milk
2 teaspoons grated ginger root
1 teaspoon honey
dash pepper

Simmer together about 10 minutes. Cool. Stir in 1 cup half and half. Chill. Serve with carrot curls. Serves 4-6.

This recipe comes from Rose Davis, a client from Hawaii.

BLACK BEAN SOUP

1 pound black beans
2 quarts water
1 teaspoon soda
1/2 cup oil
2 chopped green peppers
1 large onion
5 cloves garlic
1/2 teaspoon ground cumin
1 1/2 teaspoon oregano leaves
1 tablespoon salt

Cook beans for 2 1/2 hours. Add soda after about 1 hour and more liquid if needed.

In large skillet heat and saute in oil, green peppers, onion and garlic. Then add ground cumin, oregano leaves and salt. Simmer 30 minutes, then add lite rum or lemon juice and rice. Simmer for 30 minutes or until the rice is cooked.

To serve: add bacon, crisp and crumbled, and chopped hard boiled eggs.

THAI CURRIED SEAFOOD SOUP

2 tablespoons vegetable oil
1 large green onion
4 teaspoons minced peeled fresh
   ginger
1 tablespoon curry powder
1 1/2 teaspoons minced red jalapeño
   chili with seeds (I used one dry)
2 1/2 cups canned unsweetened
   coconut milk (available in Asian
   markets)
1/2 cup white rice
1/2 teaspoon grated lime peel
can of small clams
can of cooked shrimp,
1/3 pound bay scallops
8 fresh chives, chopped for garnish

METHOD: Heat oil in a heavy 4 quart Dutch oven. Add green onion, ginger and curry and the jalapeño and saute 5 minutes. Stir in coconut milk, clam juice, rice and bring to boil. Reduce heat and cover and simmer until rice is tender, about 15 minutes. Mix in lime juice and peel. Add clams, shrimp, and scallops and simmer for about 10 minutes. Ladle into bowls and garnish with chives.

VEGETARIAN CHILI

Assemble ingredients before you begin or this takes all day!

Chop up:
2 cups celery
2 green peppers
1 large onion
4 garlic cloves

Brown all these things in 3 tablespoons of olive oil.

Add:
48 ounces of tomatoes also chopped (canned is fine)
1 1 pound package of red beans (already cooked)
1/2 cup white raisins
a few shakes of red wine vinegar

Add all the following spices:
2 tablespoons chili powder
2 tablespoons minced parsley
2 teaspoons salt
2 teaspoons each cumin, oregano, and basil
1 teaspoon allspice (don't leave this out)
1/2 teaspoon white pepper
tabasco (a couple of good shakes)
1 bay leaf
1 botttle of beer

Let all cook together for at least an hour. This can be made a day or two in advance, then just before serving add another bottle of beer and heat for about 30 minutes. Serve with salted cashew nuts or pecans and grated Swiss cheese.

This recipe comes to me from Harold Hoiland, one of our clients from D.C., a T.V. cameraman, who loves to cook.

IOWA CORN CHOWDER

In a large kettle brown:
1 pound of bacon cut into pieces (drain on paper towels and set aside)
Pour off nearly all the fat and brown 1 large chopped onion in the remaining bacon fat. Add 8 large potatoes, peeled and cubed, and 1 tablespoon of salt. Add enough water to cover potatoes and cook for 20 minutes. When the potatoes are soft add 2 packages frozen corn (use fresh if you can get it).

Add 1 pint of table cream or 1/2 and 1/2 and enough milk to make a light soup. Serve with bacon bits, chopped green and red pepper, hot green chilis and green onion well chopped. Add these to the cup just before serving. Sprinkle cheddar cheese on top of the cup. Serve corn chowder with Corn Fritters and Honey Butter, in Bits and Bobs section.

CHICKEN AND WILD RICE SOUP

1 whole chicken
1 large onion
1 8 oz. package of wild rice, rinsed
1 tablespoon salt
1/2 teaspoon fresh pepper
1 pound sliced mushrooms
1 pint 1/2 and 1/2 or table cream
herbs for flavor
green onion
parsley

METHOD: In a large pot cover the chicken amply with water, add onion, salt and pepper (a bouquet garni of spices basil, thyme, rosemary etc. may be added). Cook the chicken on a simmer for about 3 hours. Cool, but save the broth, and cut up the chicken meat and return to the pot. Just one hour before serving add the wild rice. About 15 minutes before serving add mushrooms and cream. Simmer gently until all is blended, but do not boil at this point. Just before serving add freshly chopped parsley and green onion in the serving bowl, ladle in the hot soup.

BONNIE'S BISON AND BLACK BEAN SOUP

3 pounds ground bison meat
1 large white onion
1 tablespoon salt
2 cans black beans
1 can tomato paste (small)
2 cans chopped tomatoes
1 large can pureed tomatoes in
   chunks (can use 4 cans chopped
   tomatoes)
1 can tomato puree
1-2 pints of water
1 tablespoon oregano
4 tablespoons hot chili powder
2-3 hot red chilies
1/2 teaspoon cayenne pepper
1 can beer

METHOD: Brown onion in a little olive oil. Brown meat. Add all the spices and cook together about 1/2 hour with meat and onion. Add tomatoes and black beans and simmer for about another hour. Just before serving add the beer and bring to last boil. Bison meat can be ordered from: M & S Meats, 406-844-3414. They will send a brochure. Serves 12 people or makes a 5 quart kettle.

GRANDMA GRIFFITH'S CHILI

2 pounds ground beef
1 large onion, chopped
2 cloves garlic, chopped
4 cans white and red beans (2 each)
2 cans pinto beans
1 large can tomato sauce
2 large cans chopped tomatoes
1 large can tomato paste
1 tablespoon sugar
1 tablespoon salt
ample ground pepper
1 teaspoon white pepper
about 4 large tablespoons hot chili
   powder

This makes a 5 quart kettle full of chili and serves 8-10 people. Serve with a crusty bread.

SAUCES

BLENDER HOLLANDAISE SAUCE

1 1/2 tablespoons lemon juice
3 egg yolks
3/4 cup melted butter
1/2 teaspoon salt
1/2 teaspoon cayenne
1 teaspoon prepared mustard

Let egg yolks and lemon juice stand at room temperature, 2 hours. Heat blender container with hot water, then leave 1 tablespoon hot water in blender. Add egg yolks. Pour melted butter in very slowly, 5 seconds. Add: salt, cayenne, prepared mustard, and last, lemon juice.

SHRIMP COCKTAIL SAUCE

1 cup catsup
3 dashes tabasco
juice from 1/2" lemon slice
1 tablespoon diced green onions
1/2 stalk celery, finely chopped
1 tablespoon chili sauce
1 teaspoon horseradish
1 tablespoon sugar

Mix all together and let blend before using with shrimp.

WHITE RAVIOLI SAUCE

2 sticks butter
2 cartons sour cream
1 cup parmesan cheese
salt and pepper to taste

Melt the butter until bubbly, then add two cartons of sour cream and the parmesan cheese. Blend until warmed through and the butter is incorporated. Serve immediately over ravs or any pasta, angel hair, fettucini, or linguini.

DILL SAUCE

1/2 cup sugar
1 cup fresh dill
1 cup dijon mustard
1/2 cup white wine vinegar
1/2 cup Best Foods mayonnaise
2 tablespoons oil

METHOD: Combine all ingredients except oil in a blender. Blend until smooth. While blender is running add oil, a little at a time. Store in a glass jar. Serve with poached salmon or any shell fish.

BLACK SESAME SAUCE

4 tablespoons mayonnaise
3 tablespoons salad oil
1" ginger-grated
vinegar or lemon
enough dark sesame oil to make a
   sauce

This recipe comes from Jim Oblak.

RED SAUCE FOR PASTA

1 tablespoon olive oil
2 pounds sweet Italian sausage
   (skin removed)
6 cloves garlic, minced
1 large onion

Add:
large can tomato paste
large can pureed tomatoes
large can tomato sauce
salt & pepper
1/2 cup finely shredded fresh basil
sprig of oregano
sprig of thyme

This sauce can be used with any pasta, but I prefer Butte ravioli or penne.

Brown sweet Italian Sausage. Simmer this sauce for several hours adding a little red wine as it thickens.

Plum Sauce

Use a pan full of tart plums, pits removed, and add a little honey or sugar, hot mustard, fresh slivered ginger, and 5 spice (a Chinese spice available in most food stores.) You add all these things to suit your individual taste.

Bonnie's Plum Sauce

(a variation)
2 # tart plums (fresh off the tree is best)
1 cup apricot preserves
1 cup peach preserves
1 cup applesauce
2 teaspoons dry mustard
1 teaspoon garlic powder
1/2 cup chili sauce

Remove pits from plums and cook until soft. Puree them in the blender. In a large pan add the rest of the ingredients (Grated fresh ginger can also be added at this stage, about a one inch piece), mix together, and then cook until well blended. Put up in 1/2 pint jars about 3/4 full and freeze.

This is a year's supply for Tom and me and the wilderness trips.

Ravioli Sauce

2 pounds Italian Sausage
4 cloves garlic, chopped
1 large onion chopped
2 cans chopped tomatoes
1 large can tomato sauce
1 large can tomato paste
2 tablespoons Italian herbs
mushrooms
green parsley (fresh)

Brown the sausage and add the rest of the ingredients, simmer for the afternoon. Place over cooked ravioli and sprinkle with parmesan cheese.

Hot Mocha

1 cup cocoa
2 cups sugar
2 cups dry milk
2 cup non-dairy creamer
1/2 cup instant coffee

Use 3 tablespoons of this mixture in a mug of boiling water.

Toffee Bars

1 cup butter
1 cup brown sugar
1 teaspoon vanilla
2 cups sifted flour
1 cup chocolate chips
1/2 to 1 cup nuts

Blend butter, brown sugar and vanilla. Add flour, mix well. Add chocolate chips and nuts. Press into jelly roll pan.

Bake 350 degrees for 25 minutes.

Seasoned Salt

1/2 cup salt
1 teaspoon dry mustard
3/4 teaspoon oregano
1/2 teaspoon garlic powder
1/4 teaspoon onion powder

Mix and store in air tight container. Use on pork or chicken.

Clam Dip Blend

8 ounce package cream cheese
1 1/2 teaspoons sour cream
3/4 teaspoon salt
dash of ground pepper
1 1/2 teaspoons lemon juice
1 can minced clams (drained)
1 or 2 tablespoons clam juice from
the can (Use enough of juice to
make the consistency you like)

Make ahead so flavors blend. Take out of refrigerator in advance so it softens up. If you use more cheese, add bit more of everything, except clams, to your taste.

Caramel Fruit Dip

1 large package cream cheese
3/4 cup brown sugar
1 teaspoon vanilla

Put in microwave for 1 1/2 min. on high. Beat with electric mixer until smooth. Then add vanilla.
Store in the refrigerator.

This recipe comes from Bobbie Thompson of Omaha, NE.

Chocolate Sauce

2 squares unsweetened chocolate /
cut in small pieces
1/2 cup sugar
6 tablespoons canned milk, heated
1/2 teaspoon vanilla
dash salt
1 tablespoon butter

Mix in blender on high.

DILL PICKLES
(GRANDMA GRIFFITH'S)

3 quarts water
1 quart vinegar
scant cup salt
1/2 teaspoon
alum
3"- 4" cucumbers

Put lots of garlic cloves in the jars at least 5-6. One dill sprig of fresh dill or 2 tablespoons dill seed. Water bath for 10 minutes.

WHITNEY CRAB PICKLES

10 cups sugar
1 cup vinegar
1/2 cup water (no more)

Bring to boil slowly. Put apples in and boil 5 minutes. Hot water bath for 10 minutes. This is a very loose recipe. I use one 5 quart kettle nearly full of the apples for this much sauce. It makes about 7 pints.

FRESH PRUNE CHUTNEY

1 cup light brown sugar, firmly
 packed
1 cup granulated sugar
3/4 cup cider vinegar
1 1/2 teaspoon crushed red peppers
2 teaspoons mustard seed
2 cloves garlic, thinly sliced
1/3 cup thin sliced onion
1/2 cup thin sliced preserved ginger
1 cup seedless white raisins
3 1/2 cups fresh Italian prunes,
 halved and seeded.

Mix together sugars and vinegar, bring to boiling point. Add remaining ingredients except prunes. Mix well. Stir in prunes. Simmer until thickened - about 50 minutes, stirring frequently and gently. Fill sterilized jars and seal or freeze.
Use on toast or onion bagels, top with cream cheese - then chutney!

Beef Jerky

2 pounds flank steak (cut 1/4" strips
with grain-length of steak)
1 1/2 teaspoons ground pepper
1 teaspoon sodium glutamate
1 teaspoon onion powder
1/4 cup soy sauce
1/4 cup Worcestershire Sauce

Marinate flank steak overnight. Bake at 175 degree, 6 hours or overnight. This is a backpacker's companion.

Salami

5 pounds any burger
5 rounded teaspoons Morton's tender
quick salt
2 1/2 teaspoons whole mustard seed
5 teaspoons whole peppercorns
cracked
2 1/2 teaspoons garlic powder
2 1/2 teaspoons liquid smoke
1 1/2 teaspoons crushed red pepper
2 1/2 teaspoons salt

Mix: Cover overnight, mix like that for 4 days - on 4th day, roll out in 4 salami, put them on a cookie sheet. Bake 140 degrees for 8 hours, turn it occasionally, or just bake overnight.

This is a recipe for wild game meat essentially, given to me by an avid Montana hunter.

Glazed Fresh Fruit

2 cups sugar
1 cup water
1 teaspoon cream of tartar

Bring to boil stirring constantly to hard ball stage, 250 degrees. Dip fruits into it 1 piece at time and put in cool dry place on greased (well oiled cookie sheet) (strawberries, grapes, pear chunks, peach chunks, apple wedges with peel, tangerine sections,) dry on towels before you dip in sugar syrup.

BATTER FOR FISH FRY

Batter:
2 eggs
1 or 2 tablespoons cornstarch
soy sauce (several drops)

Dip:
1/4 cup flour
1/4 cup instant potato flakes
1 tablespoon cornmeal
1 teaspoon salt
1 teaspoon pepper

Prepare batter. Mix dry ingredients with fork. Dip fish in batter and then in a mixture of the dry ingredients. Deep fat fry.

TEMPERA BATTER FOR FISH

Beat 1 egg

add:
1/2 cup flour and enough milk to make a thin, smooth batter, chill until ready to cook, fry fish in this batter.

BEET PICKLES

2 cups vinegar
1 cup sugar
2 sticks cinnamon
1/2 teaspoon cloves (whole)

Put spices in sack and place in vinegar and sugar to boil for 5 minutes. Pour over hot cooked beats in sterilized jars and seal. Hot water bath for 10 minutes.

Hot Cocoa Mix

12 quarts powdered milk
2 cups powdered sugar
32 ounces Nestles Quick Chocolate
12 ounces coffeemate

Mix all together and store in an airtight tin. Use 3 heaping tablespoons to one mug of boiling water. You can add some powdered coffee crystals to make a Mocha drink.

Piña Colada

6 ounce can pineapple juice
4 ounces canned coconut milk
4 tablespoons coconut syrup
Juice of 1 lime
4 ounces cream
5 ounces light rum

Put in blender - add 2 cups crushed ice - blend until ice is fine.

Peanut Butterscotch Crunch

1/2 cup crunchy peanut butter
12 ounces butterscotch morsels
6 cups corn flakes

Melt peanut butter and butterscotch morsels together over low heat. Add corn flakes to mixture. Drop off teaspoon onto waxed paper.

Makes 75 pieces

CORN FRITTERS

2 cups fresh or frozen corn
4 beaten eggs
1 cup flour
1/2 teaspoon salt
1 teaspoon baking powder
2 tablespoons sugar

If you whirl the corn in the processor, it gives the fritters more flavor. Sift dry ingredients. Add eggs and corn. Drop from teaspoon into hot fat, 370 degrees. Fry until light brown. They will flop over in the pan by themselves (we used to love to watch this in my grandmother's kitchen.) Serve hot with smooth delicious Honey Butter.

HONEY BUTTER

In blender or beater bowl break 1/2 cup butter into small pieces. Add 1 cup liquid honey, warmed. Blend for a few seconds. Makes about 2 cups.

This is delicious with rolls, pancakes and other goodies as well.

BRANDIED APRICOT JELLY

3 1/2 cups sugar
1/2 cup Brandy
1 1/2 cup apricot nectar
2 tablespoons lemon juice (fresh)

Stir until sugar is dissolved. Remove and add 1/2 bottle Certo. Mix well, pour into sterile jars and seal.

Sandy Mueller's Sweet Pickles

These ingredients are for 1 gallon of cukes 3-4 inches long.

Day 1: Wash cukes and put in large crock. Cover with 1 gallon of water and 1 cup of pickling salt. Put a plate on top of the cukes so they stay under water. Cover with a cloth. Let stand one week. Seven (7) days later - drain and cover with boiling water and 2 tablespoons of powdered alum. Let stand 24 hours. The next morning drain and split the pickles into chunks-cover with boiling water and let stand 24 hours.

The following morning drain them and boil together:
2 quarts of sugar
1 quart of apple cider vinegar
2 tablespoons of pickling spices
1/4 teaspoon mace
4 sticks of cinnamon (don't substitute ground cinnamon)

Pour this over the pickles and let stand for 24 hours. Heat juices to boiling and pour over pickles 3 more days. 4th morning seal them in pints that are scalding hot. Cover with boiling hot juices from the pickles. Seal tightly. Process 5 minutes in a boiling water bath. Be sure to pack the pickles as tightly as possible in the jars.

GENERAL INDEX

4 C's Potatoes 110
Almond Roca Cookies................................ 74
Anchovy Bread... 4
Antipasto Pasta Salad............................... 90
Apple Pie 79
Apple Torte 53
Apricot Brandied Brie 2
Apricot Horns... 21
Apricot Nuggets....................................... 59
Artichoke and Tarragon Dip........................ 2
Artichoke Nibbles 8
Baked Chicken 120
Baked Chicken Breasts............................ 128
Banana Bar Frosting................................. 59
Banana Bars.. 59
Banana Bread 18
Bara Brith (Welsh Bread)........................... 13
Batter for Fish Fry................................... 150
BBQ Drumettes 3
BBQ Ribs 115
Beef Bites 3
Beef Jerky 149
Beer Waffles 36
Beet Pickles 150
Best Ever Zucchini Bread 16
Best Zucchini Bars 63
Better Than Robert Redford Cake.............. 51
Birds Nests 68
Black Bean Soup 137
Black Bottom Cupcakes 42
Black Sesame Sauce 143
Blender Hollandaise Sauce 142
Bonnie's Bison and Black Bean Soup......... 140
Bonnie's Napoleons.................................. 88
Bonnie's Plum Sauce............................... 144
Bonnie's White Sauce Fettuccine.............. 122
Boursin Cheese 5
Bran Oat Muffins 30
Brandied Apricot Jelly.............................. 152
Brandied Mushrooms 4
Breakfast Muffins 29
Breakfast Sausage Bake 24
Broccoli with Sesame and Lemon 106
Butter Crunch Pie Crust 86
Butter Egg Frosting 41
Buttercreams for Christmas 71
Butterfly Cakes 39
Butterhorn Rolls 17

Butterhorn Rolls Frosting 17
Cabbage Slaw... 97
Caramel Fruit Dip.................................... 147
Carrot Bar Frosting................................... 66
Carrot Bars... 66
Carrot Cake.. 57
Cheese and Meat Bread 23
Chewy Pecan Cookies 60
Chick Pea Soup with Garlic and Herbs...... 132
Chicken and Barley Soup......................... 130
Chicken and Wild Rice Soup.................... 139
Chicken Cider Stew 118
Chicken Fruit Salad................................. 99
Chicken Soup with Corn Tortillas.............. 131
Chicken Wings 6
Chinese Chicken Salad 91
Chinese Cole Slaw.................................. 100
Chocolate Cashew Toffee 64
Chocolate Frosting 45
Chocolate Mayonnaise Cake...................... 41
Chocolate Mint Pie 77
Chocolate Mountain Bars 60
Chocolate Nut Logs 70
Chocolate Nut Pie 77
Chocolate Praline Cake............................. 58
Chocolate Raspberry Cake 46
Chocolate Sauce 147
Chocolate Square..................................... 44
Chocolate Upside Down Cake.................... 56
Chocolate Whipped Cream Frosting 48
Chocolate Zucchini Cake........................... 54
Cinnamon Rolls.. 19
Clam Dip Blend...................................... 147
Coca Cola Cake....................................... 40
Coca Cola Icing....................................... 40
Coconut Chicken Soup............................ 133
Cold Carrot Ginger Soup 136
Cold Dilled Peas 107
Corn Fritters 152
Cornish Game Hens 117
Cornish Pasties 127
Crab Meat Parmesan Canapes..................... 2
Crab Rounds... 3
Cream Cheese Bars 66
Cream Cheese Coffee Cake........................ 26
Cream Sherry Bundt Cake......................... 40
Creamy Mushroom and Chicken Soup...... 132
Crumpets.. 12

GENERAL INDEX (CONT'D)

Crunchy Vegetable Salad............................ 90
Decadent Chocolate Cookies...................... 72
Deep South Baked Chicken 128
Devils Food Cake 45
Dill Pickles.. 148
Dill Sauce... 143
Do-Ahead Bran Muffins 29
Don Walter's Broccoli Salad...................... 100
Don Walter's Sweet Potato Salad.............. 105
Easy Apple Pie.. 86
Egg Noodles... 135
Eggplant Lasagne 125
Fettuccine Romana 119
Flour Tortilla 15
Four Cheese Soup..................................... 133
French Silk Chocolate Tarts 87
Fresh Prune Chutney................................. 148
Frosted Creams 65
Fruit Salad Dressing.................................. 96
Fruit Salad Dressing.................................. 98
Frystekake... 50
Giant Muffin Mix 37
Ginger Shrimp Appetizer 8
Ginger, Lemon and Walnut Muffins 32
Glazed Fresh Fruit..................................... 149
Glazed Peach Pie 85
Glazed Raspberry Pie................................. 83
Gooey Butter Cake.................................... 54
Grain Bread 13
Grandma Griffith's Chili............................. 140
Grandma Griffith's Coleslaw...................... 102
Grandma Griffith's Potato Salad 102
Grandma's Special-Tea Cookies.................. 43
Grape Nuts Bread 14
Greek Chops 114
Green Bean Bundles 107
Green Beans Caesar 93
Ham 123
Hap's Greeny Meany Jello.......................... 94
Hap's New Cheesecake 47
Hasselback Potatoes 106
Hawaiian Pie... 85
Homemade Syrup...................................... 24
Honey Baked Apples 76
Honey Butter 152
Hot Brie Appetizer 6
Hot Chicken Salad En Casserole................. 103
Hot Cocoa Mix 151
Hot Mocha.. 146

Hundred Dollar Cake 52
Iowa Corn Chowder 139
Iowa Cucumber Salad 104
Iowa Dump Cake 50
Israeli Brownies 69
King Salmon Chowder 130
Layered Salad.. 101
Lefse 15
Lemon Bars... 78
Lemon Chicken.. 120
Lemon Pancakes 28
Lin Lee's French Silk Pie............................ 76
Make Ahead Mashed Potatoes.................. 110
Mandarin Lettuce Salad............................. 95
Maple Bacon Oven Pancake...................... 25
Marinated Mushrooms 6
Mashed Potatoes Cabbage
  and Cheddar Cheese............................... 108
Mashed Potatoes with Caramelized Onions
  and Cabbage 108
Meatball Soup 136
Mee's Cake 38
Minestrone Soup....................................... 131
Miracle Cobbler... 78
Mississippi Potatoes 109
Monster Cookies 62
Montana Cowboy Cookies 61
No Roll Pie Crust 81
Noodle Pudding 114
Noreen's Chocolate Chip Icing................... 41
Norwegian Apple Pudding......................... 89
Norwegian Coffee Ring.............................. 14
Norwegian Meatballs for a Crowd............. 123
Nut Goodie Bars 67
Nutty Pumpkin Muffins............................. 34
Oat Bran Apple Muffins 31
Oat Bran Muffins 30
Oatmeal Muffins....................................... 35
Oil Pie Crust 81
Old English Fruit Cake............................... 55
Old Fashioned Sour Cream Raisin Pie......... 80
Onion Butter... 7
Onion Party Puffs 7
Orange and Chocolate Muffins 32
Orange Lemon Pie 84
Orange Oatmeal Muffins............................ 33
Orange Rolls 11
Oven Baked Chicken................................. 121
Oven Puff Pancake.................................... 25

GENERAL INDEX (CONT'D)

Overnight Cookie 69
Pancakes 28
Pasta Salad or Vegetable Salad 92
Pastry Puffs 8
Peanut Butter Pie 82
Peanut Butterscotch Crunch 151
Pears Poached in Red Wine 76
Pecan Pie 84
Pie Crust Mix 81
Piña Colada 151
Pineapple Oatmeal Muffins 33
Plum Sauce 144
Poppy Seed Dressing 96
Poppyseed Bread 19
Pork Stew with Mushrooms
   and White Wine 113
Potato Bites 5
Potato, Lentil and Mushroom Soup 134
Potatoes for a Crowd 109
Pots d' Creme 83
Pumpkin Bars 73
Pumpkin Bread 14
Pumpkin Nut Muffins 37
Quesadillas 126
Quick Sorbet 83
Ranch Dressing 96
Ravioli Sauce 144
Ready in the Morning Yeast Waffles 36
Red Sauce for Pasta 143
Reeses' Peanut Butter Bars 73
Refreshing Summer Pasta Salad 91
Refrigerator Bran Muffins 31
Refrigerator Coleslaw 104
Refrigerator Potato Bread 20
Rhubarb Cake 49
Rice Cookies 74
Roasted Eggplant Dip 9
Robin Johnson's Butterscotch Pie 89
Russian Buns 22
Salami 149
Salmon Salad 104
Sandy Mueller's Sweet Pickles 153
Sausage Filled Crepes 122
Sausage Onion Soup Uptown Cafe 134
Sausage Puffs 4
Sausage Roll 9
Scotched Bacon Chestnut Appetizer 7
Scottish Oat Scones 26

Seasoned Salt 146
Sesame Dressing 97
Sesame Seed Salad 98
Shrimp Cocktail Sauce 142
Simple Muffin Mix 35
Sis Polin's Brisket 118
Sis Polin's Easy Potato Knishes 121
Slaw Dressing (Gram) 95
Sour Cream Chocolate Chip Cookies 68
Sourdough Hot Cakes 27
Spaetzle 135
Spicy Cauliflower 92
Spicy Pot Roast 112
Spinach and Chicken Enchiladas 116
Stan Watt's Franchisable Pizza 124
Strawberry Bread 18
Strawberry Pie 85
Stuffed Mushrooms 5
Sugar Cookies 63
Swedish Pancakes 24
Sweet and Sour Green Beans 107
Sweet Milk Doughnuts 12
Taco Filling 117
Tart Shells 87
Tempera Batter for Fish 150
Thai Curried Seafood Soup 137
Thousand Island Dressing 98
Three Green Pasta with Scallops
   and Pesto Sauce 112
Toasty Oat Granola 34
Toffee Bars 146
Torte Lemon Dessert 82
Triple Chocolate Cake 51
Vanilla Pudding Dessert 88
Vegetarian Chili 138
Whipped Cream Dressing 99
Whiskey Balls 74
White Bean Salad 93
White Ravioli Sauce 142
Whitney Crab Pickles 148
Whitver's Lime Jello 94
Whole Wheat Egg Bread 10
Zucchini Pancakes 27

Books by Tom Murphy

Silence and Solitude
9 x 12 hardcover with dust jacket, 128 pages, full color photographs, published by Riverbend Publishing, Helena, Montana, $29.95

In **Silence and Solitude: Yellowstone's Winter Wilderness** Tom Murphy shows us the splendor and force of Yellowstone's long, cold winter. Through stunning photography we begin to feel the inspiring power of a landscape still wild and pure.

The Light of Spring
11 x 12 hardcover with dust jacket, 148 pages, full color photographs, published by Crystal Creek Press, Livingston, Montana, $35.00

The Light of Spring: The Seasons of Yellowstone is the first of a four volume set by Tom Murphy called **The Seasons of Yellowstone.** The turning of a full year in Yellowstone Park includes four distinct seasons. Each one flows and overlaps the next one but has its own unique character. Spring's uniqueness comes from the powerful pulse of light warming the land. It starts and maintains the growth of vegetation and supports the birth of a myriad of creatures.

The Comfort of Autumn: The Seasons of Yellowstone
11 x 12 hardcover with dust jacket, 148 pages, full color photographs, published by Crystal Creek Press, Livingston, Montana, $35.00

This book takes the reader to Autumn in Yellowstone with its great beauty. Autumn brings maturation and independence for the young animals, the rut and mating season for many large mammals, and the drive to put on fat for the coming winter. It is the time for the seeding of plants and starting the process of dormancy for trees, bushes, grasses, and forbs.

The Abundance of Summer: The Seasons of Yellowstone
11 x 12 hardcover with dust jacket, 148 pages, full color photographs, published by Crystal Creek Press, Livingston, Montana, $40.00

The summer book, is the most recent and 3rd book in the four part series about the seasons of Yellowstone. Summer is defined by the growth of the wildlife and luxuriant flora in the Park. The long warm days and cool nights make it the most pleasant and easy season.

Next in the series, due out in 2011 will be the book about the winter season in Yellowstone. There will be a slipcover available for the set of four. Photographers from around the world have collected this series both for its instructional value and for its beauty.

Copies may be purchased from the Tom Murphy website: tmurphywild.com.

Wilderness Photography Expeditions
402 South 5th Street
Livingston, Montana 59047
Phone (406) 222-2302 or (406) 222-2986
tom@tmurphywild.com or bhyattmurphy@mcn.net